# The Amazing Lamb of God

## Exciting Secrets for His Younger Lambs

# Matthew 18

*The Greatest in the Kingdom of Heaven*

**18** At that time the disciples came to Jesus and asked, "Who is the greatest in the kingdom of heaven?"

[2] He called a little child and had him stand among them. [3] And He said: "I tell you the truth, unless you change and become like little children, you will never enter the kingdom of heaven. [4] Therefore, whoever humbles himself like this child is the greatest in the kingdom of heaven. [5] And whoever welcomes a little child like this in My name welcomes Me.

# The Amazing Lamb of God

Exciting Secrets for His
Younger Lambs

*Dr. Richard E. Eby*
Illustrated by Judith Cheng

Personal communications and collected papers from the author's father, the late Eugene D. Eby, electrical engineer and Bible scholar, were useful in organizing much of the story material for *The Amazing Lamb of God*.

Unless otherwise identified, Scripture quotations in this volume are from the HOLY BIBLE, NEW INTERNATIONAL VERSION, copyright © 1978, 1984, New York International Bible Society. Used by permission of Zondervan Bible Publishers.

Scripture quotations identified KJV are from the King James Version.

Scripture quotations identified TEV are from the *Good News Bible*—Old Testament: Copyright © American Bible Society 1976: New Testament: Copyright © American Bible Society 1966, 1971, 1976.

Verses marked TLB are taken from *The Living Bible*, Copyright ©1971 by Tyndale House Publishers, Wheaton, Ill. Used by permission.

Selected words within quoted Scriptures are capitalized or italicized for emphasis and alternate readings are supplied in parentheses to clarify the meaning for young readers. Synonyms for Hebrew and Greek words were selected with the aid of *Strong's Exhaustive Concordance of the Bible*.

Take note that the name satan and related names are not capitalized. We choose not to acknowledge him, even to the point of violating grammatical rules.

## Treasure House

An Imprint of
**Destiny Image**
**P.O. Box 310**
**Shippensburg, PA 17257**

"For where your treasure is
there will your heart be also." Matthew 6:21

ISBN 1-56043-803-7

For Worldwide Distribution
Printed in the U.S.A.

Treasure House books are available through these fine distributors outside the United States:

Christian Growth, Inc.
Jalan Kilang-Timor, Singapore 0315

Lifestream
Nottingham, England

Rhema Ministries Trading
Randburg, South Africa

Salvation Book Centre
Petaling, Jaya, Malaysia

Successful Christian Living
Capetown, Rep. of South Africa

Vision Resources
Ponsonby, Auckland, New Zealand

WA Buchanan Company
Geebung, Queensland, Australia

Word Alive
Niverville, Manitoba, Canada

# Dedication

To the thousands of babies who kept their parents and me from sleeping regular hours I present this little story about God's loving Lamb. Many of "my babies" are now grown up, and have already qualified as diaper-changers, bottle washers, and midnight walkers. Some are grandparents who now can love little dears, not lug them.

For all of them, our Father in Heaven has the ultimate answer to every problem: "Love one another as I have loved you." You are all potential "Lord's Lambs." I love you.

Our Most High God called my wife, Maybelle, to her heavenly home in Paradise on September 16, 1986. Though we shall be one *in* Him at the rapture, still I dedicate this to her...

To my ever-loving Maybelle goes my eternal appreciation for her living example of commitment. During my "practice" days she was left alone much of the time to run the family affairs, to be both mother and father to the children.

During my "ministry" days she again spent lonesome weeks keeping the home fires burning when her failing sight prevented her from traveling.

During my "writing" days she graciously endured loneliness while sharing equal time with a typewriter!

Never once did she complain, knowing that whatever blessings may come to the readers of our little books about God's love will be multiplied into heavenly treasures—forever.

Thank you, Honey, for *our* love affair!

# Contents

**Promises from the Father Above**

# To My Little Ones
# on Earth

Give Me your ear
My little one,
I gave My all,
I gave My Son!

Before you wake
My little one,
Your day I make,
I bring you sun!

I give you strength
My little one,
I smooth the path
so you can run!

I'll heal your hurts
My little one,
Just come and ask,
you'll find it's done!

When you must fight
My little one,
I go ahead—
your battle's won!

This is My plan
daughter or son,
Believe in Me—
that makes us one!

The Lamb of God
bids you to come,
Of such on earth
is His Kingdom!

Amen.

# Preface

The greatest love story is still new to each generation. In retelling, it grows sweeter as the days go by. All children need to hear it, even if they are already "grown-ups." Parents should tell it to children because God said so. It is His story, the first true Love Story.

His Book says that He made people into parents to share with them the kind of love that *He* has for *His* children. Besides He needs their help, to retell His Good News.

God's ancient shepherd Moses said that God promises children a long life if they will honor father and mother. Parents are to tell them about the heavenly Father before youngsters even learn to read. God expects that there will be a "listening hour" every day for them to hear about the exciting Love Story God has planned for them.

God knew that His true stories would be Good News for everyone who listened. They tell of love and abundant life, of victory over defeat, of strength to replace weakness, of dreams that can come true, of peace instead of terror, of joy to replace sorrow, and above all, of a Savior instead of a satan! Jesus said *His* words are *life*.

To parents and children alike Jesus gives this sacred promise:

*See, the Sovereign Lord comes with power, and His arm rules for Him. See, His reward is with Him, and His recompense accompanies Him. He tends His flock like a shepherd: He gathers the lambs in His arms and carries them close to His heart; He gently leads those that have young.*

Isaiah 40:10-11

Only one promise can finally exceed that one. The Lamb says:

*Behold, I come quickly: blessed is he that keepeth the sayings of the prophecy of this book.* Revelation 22:7 KJV

The *greatest story* begins and ends with the Lamb!

Part One of this Love Story describes God's secret plans of long ago. The exciting wisdom of God was a mystery to men of old. Out of clouds and burning bushes and pillars of fire, He spoke to His prophets by day. At night He used dreams and visions. He even wrote on stones, or sent angels to speak and even wrestle with people. He often fought battles for His people by using trumpet blasts, singing soldiers, and invisible hosts of armed angels. God even predicted a Messiah—someday!

All of the things God did for His children were "previews" or preparations for the coming of Christ Jesus, His Son and your Lamb.

Part Two reveals how this "last generation" receives God's answers to His secret plans. The Messiah came to earth, right on schedule, to fulfill the prophecies from God, to explain the secrets, and become a *revealing Lamb*:

*...the revelation of the mystery hidden for long ages past, but now revealed and made known...so that all nations might believe and obey Him.* Romans 16:25-26

Before Jesus came, your Father laid His gifts and promises away on the shelf. When Jesus came down from Heaven, He took the Lay-Away Gifts off the shelf of God's storehouse and relabeled them Give-Away Gifts. Then Jesus said: "Ask, and it shall be given you." What a glorious idea!

# Background 1919

**A**few frightening months earlier World War I had ended. We had heard the whistles blowing at the distant factory over the hill, and church bells clanging for hours, even though it wasn't Sunday! Dad had told us kids that we now were at peace. We scowled: Peace, what's that? Ever since we were old enough to remember, people said we were at war. They said it was far away: "Thank God," they added. "Our men are over *there* fighting for freedom." (Our neighbors had usually looked sad and seldom came to visit.)

But this day my brother and I were aware that the ladies from town were happy as they sat with Mom on our porch at Castle Windy. We could hear them laugh as they swapped plans to get one of those new crank-up phones with the bells on top, or better yet a "Tin Lizzie" to replace Ol' Dobbin on those long trips into town.

On summer days like this we children were left free to romp through the fields of timothy grass and daisies that lined the Pontoosuc lakeshore in the Berkshire Hills. Our three little guests would shriek with glee as the grasshoppers and frogs leaped away in panic. Then we would stop to catch our breath, and flop laughing into the sweet-smelling patch of clover under a handy white birch shade tree.

For a moment no one would speak. Up there in the sky hung huge frosty pillows with feathery edges.

Shadowy streaks appeared to fall through them down toward the mountains around the lake. These clouds seemed suspended on unseen wires from the blueness above. We were immediately lost in wonderment while our imaginations re-formed each shape into castles full of kings and things.

"Little Bert'a" was the first to speak. Being only four, she had learned the hard way that she must speak first or not get a chance before the "old guys" would say, "Be Quiet!" (or worse). With authority she announced: "Thass where Jethus liffs! If I wath Him, I would make thum ithe cream and haff a partee!"

"Oh yeah?" her brother Ed snorted, "If *you* was God, the sky would fall down! When *I* grow up and get rich, I'll eat all the ice cream I want—with chocolate over it. You'll see!"

I wondered what my little six-year-old brother Bob would say about ice cream; it was his favorite food—anytime. Right now he seemed far away as he squinted aloft. "Yeah, ice cream's alright, but wouldn't it be fun to be God? I could have anything I want, especially someone to do my chores. I hate weeding! Yeah, I could buy myself a flashlight and look for angels at night! Mom says they sleep around me. I could look under the bed with a flashlight. Wow! If I was God, I could open my mouth and have thunder come out—like He does. Las' night I felt Him shake the ground while He was watering it."

Bob paused to look over his elbow at the rest of us. "Mom says not to be afraid of anything that God does. She says His thunder is just to get our attention to say

He loves children best. I told her that's a funny way to love *me*! She says He has other ways too. Does *your* mother talk to you as though God is *real*?"

Bert'a was quiet this time as fourth-grader Lois sat up and hugged her knees under her chin. "Well, Momma has been telling us that Jesus loves all of us so much that *she* can't even understand it. And *she* went to college! She says that Daddy can probably explain about God better. He teaches Sunday School!" Then she giggled. "Momma says she knows more about how to love us because she is a mother; and it takes more love to do housekeeping than to go to an office every day. She's right!"

"That's what YOU think," Ed replied. "It takes brains to work in an office. Remember this morning? Dad had us all say that verse: 'My people are destroyed for lack of knowledge.' Dad's no dummy. He makes money for us at the office. Besides, he loves us too!"

Bob was listening. He kept staring at the clouds: "I guess God is like a mom and dad all at the same time. He must have so many brains that He can give everyone some. He must have lots of love too; *He* didn't spank me for sassing Mom yesterday...only Dad did. Dad's funny. He said it hurt him more than me!"

Bob paused to pull up a timothy stem and suck its sweet juice: "Yeah, if I was God I would make so much of everything that I could give it away and have lots left, like money and bicycles and fishin' poles. I would make Christmas every day...Hey, Mom's calling."

Just then, the knitting party on the porch broke up. "Lois! Bertha! Ed! Robert! Richard! Time for ice cream! Come and get it. Last one here is a slowpoke!"

That was sixty-five years ago! Those little lambs have now grown into old sheep. They are now the fathers and mothers who dish out ice cream or go to offices "to use their brains" to help *their* grandkids.

Yet God is the same. He is no older; He is still loving, teaching, and caring for them. He still calls the young and old alike, "My lambs," just as He does His Son. He wants them to talk the same language and to know each other's voices. He wants them to fall in love and follow the *same* Shepherd in order to fulfill the prayer He gave them:

Your kingdom come,
Your will be done
on earth as it is in heaven.

# Part I

# God's
# Lay-Away Plans

# Chapter 1

# The Preparations

*Abraham answered, "God Himself will **provide** the lamb for the burnt offering, my son." And the two of them went on together.*
Genesis 22:8

*To man belong the **plans** of the heart, but from the Lord comes the reply of the tongue.*
Proverbs 16:1

*You **prepare** a table before me in the presence of my enemies...*
Psalm 23:5

*O [God], **prepare** mercy and truth, which may preserve him.*
Psalm 61:7 KJV

*It was the day of **Preparation** of Passover Week, about the sixth hour, "Here is your king," Pilate said to the Jews.*
John 19:14

*Stand firm then, with the belt of truth buckled around your waist, with the breastplate of righteousness in place, and with your feet fitted with the **readiness** that comes from the gospel of peace.*
Ephesians 6:14-15

*The Lord hath **prepared** His throne in the heavens; and His kingdom ruleth over all.*
Psalm 103:19 KJV

*Instead, they were longing for a better country—a heavenly one. Therefore God is not ashamed to be called their God, for He has **prepared** a city for them.*
Hebrews 11:16

# Christmas, When God Prepared Love

Children love to go shopping before Christmas! It is such fun to get something for mom and dad, something they don't expect! A gift that says, "I love you."

In the old days before skateboards and airplanes we kids could see nothing special on sale in the downtown stores until *after* Thanksgiving. Before that we would peer hopefully through the store windows only to see the same displays which had been there since the previous New Year's. We could tell which items were the latest because they were less dusty. Yet nothing looked new; work shoes were still made with leather lacings, and the corduroy pants had the same bronze buttons, officially stamped with UNION across the Eagle.

There were rows of stiff-starched, white button-collars with pointed or rounded edges, for office or Sunday wear. Small black bow ties were lined up on a velvet covered board, accented by cuff links with pretty colored stones of different shapes. On wooden coat-stands hung the dress-up suits with their dark herringbone coats unbuttoned. We exclaimed at the two-colored gold chains (threaded through a vest buttonhole) with an initialed penknife on one end, and a pocket watch with an engraved mule deer on the other.

Our hearts sank! Would Christmas ever come? It had been so long since the last one. Last year's yellow pencils and soft brown erasers found in each of our big red stockings had been used up. We would get Mother some new clothespins.

We were anxious for the day when something for Dad would go on display. Dad was special to us all year long, but more so at Christmas. He had already given us our allowances of a penny a week for weeding the summer squash and squushing the fat tomato worms before they could strip the vines. Once in a while he would whisper as he harnessed up old Dicky-Whoa: "There will be something under your plates tonight at supper time if you gather a bouquet of brown-eyed Susans for Mother's place—from you and me." It was always another penny.

Bob and I would lose no time in secretly dropping each coin through the slot we had poked in the top of the Rumford Baking Powder can. Then the can was returned to its hiding place. The money would go for Dad's stocking present at Christmas. We hoped to have enough for a whole box of shotgun shells for his favorite fun of hunting rabbits! Wouldn't he be surprised on Christmas morning?

### Nothing Happens Without Preparation

Like most children, we simply expected that "Christmas things" would show up after Thanksgiving was over. We did not yet realize that someone always must *prepare* and *plan* in advance so that there can be a Christmas. The special decorations, the cookies, the presents, and red flannel stockings at the chimney didn't just happen!

We knew Christmas was close the day Dad got out the axe and sharpened it. As we trudged through the squeaky snow to the woodlot down the lane, he explained how God had started planning to grow us a Christmas tree billions of years ago. First, He had to make a world with just the right amount of water and soil to grow great forests and grasslands, he said. Then He put lots of ancient kinds of animals everywhere to eat the green things. The leaves and animals died and made the soil more fertile. Then He sent lightning to burn enough trees to add ashes for minerals. When the day would come for us to celebrate Jesus' Birthday, our Christmas tree would be grown, all green and six feet tall! Dad said that a tree is one of God's favorite illustrations of the need for *Preparation*.

As we dragged our tree back to the house, we could all but taste the popcorn awaiting us in bowls on the warming lid of the iron oven. Dad explained that popcorn takes *preparation* too. Some sweating farmer out west, maybe in Iowa, had guided his panting horses with flapping reins around his armpits. His calloused hands had held the rough wooden handles of the bucking plowshare. He then planted popcorn to be harvested under the burning sunshine in time to ship it east for our Christmastime snack before the warm fireplace!

As kids, we had thought that everything "just happened." Dad told us that someone's mind and heart is responsible for preparing *all* good things. "For instance," he would add, "you can see to eat your popcorn and milk tonight because someone designed and made that kerosene lamp; someone you'll never know!

Way out in Oklahoma someone worked in mud and grime to drill the oil well that produced the kerosene that burns in the wick that someone else made."

We turned to look at him. "Yes, it is true that all of us need each other. Look at my thick glasses! Without them I would not know what you look like. Do you know that a sweaty man shoveled sand into a hot furnace somewhere to make molten glass? Another man poured it into molds, and another one ground it into lenses. Then someone bent gold wires to fit over the ears, screwed it to the eyeglass, and sent it to my doctor. He fitted it to me, and I see you! Mercy, you're the best looking boys I have seen!"

We were wondering if he really had the right glasses on, because his eyes were making little tears. He bent over and hugged us so his face wouldn't show. It wasn't too hard to understand what he had meant. Brother and I already knew that Dad and Mom were necessary to us: we didn't earn our own clothes or pay the rent for a warm cottage or know how to cook strawberry shortcakes or do the laundry! Come to think of it, we didn't even pay Mom and Dad for anything they did for us. It was like a free ride, like the good things God does for us.

### "Glowing" Requires Preparation Too

The fireplace logs had burned down into a hot heap. We noticed that Dad was dreamily staring into the glowing coals. "Boys, just think of the *preparation* it took for God to keep us warm tonight! How long ago do you suppose He put that heat into that log, and how did He do it?" We shrugged.

The yellow flames flickered on his thick glasses as he turned toward us. "I suppose we'll know more about His timetable someday. Scientists tell us that logs (and everything) are made of tiny atoms and electrons that whirl around so fast that they make a log feel solid to us. When they get extra hot from spinning even faster, some parts of the atoms fly off. This makes waves that we call light. Then the light turns into heat, and the heat goes back into parts of atoms. Then everything starts all over, they say."

Dad shifted his chair nearer the fire so he could see if we were catching on. "Now let me tell you the surprising thing; these scientists tell us that *nothing* ever gets lost. After that log burns into ashes, there are just as many atoms left in the world as when the log was still there. In the meantime you and I have been enjoying the warmth and the colored flames and even the nice smell of the wood fire that God *prepared* for *us*."

We suddenly wondered, *So what*? We couldn't see any of those *atoms*, and besides there were more logs left in the woodpile outdoors. Was there more to this story?

Little wrinkles showed beside Dad's eyes. "I got ahead of you, didn't I? That's the trouble with us old folks, isn't it? You see, a burning log is not really much different from us; unless we share the warmth and light that is in us, we lie around and rot or get full of wormholes. But when we get on fire and use our stored-up energies to make life better for someone else, we become useful, and not selfish. Now run along and get ready for bed. Bring a cushion back with you because I have an exciting story to tell you before Christmas morning!"

### Dad's Christmas Eve Story

You can be sure that we jumped into our woolen nighties with the warm socks in *record* time before the fire might burn down, and a December chill take over.

We grabbed cushions from the wicker rocking chair and hurried to the fireplace. Dad was pouring his favorite drink into our three cups: sweet, steaming, Northern Spy apple cider from the ancient press by the millstream below the dam. Yummie!

A year earlier he had told us that Santa Claus was really a wonderful make believe spirit of Christmas who "borrowed" all the children around the earth to give *himself* a family at Christmastime! Of course, he knew that the *real* fathers could not let him have *all* the fun of buying presents and loving kids. So he just played "pretend" while the real dads and moms hid the gifts and goodies till Christmas day. It was then that we realized how much those "Ho Ho Ho's" last year had sounded like Dad's voice! We were sure glad that there was a Santa Claus anyway; we could be his helper, just like Dad. We liked the reindeer story too.

Dad sipped his cider before he spoke: "Do you remember the question I left unanswered an hour ago? I was asking: 'Who put the heat in that log?' Our ancestors used to call it a yule log." We remained silent. "Not everybody knows *that* truth. Let me tell you how I found out. I think you will understand if you listen *real hard*. It is an exciting discovery. It is part of what I want to call God's Lay-Away Plan!"

Just then Mom appeared in the circle of flickering firelight. Her crochet needle was sticking through a loop of her half-finished linen doily. "I see my three big men are ready to catch a reindeer before morning! Daddy, don't you think the boys should get to bed?" We could tell by her tone that she hoped he would say *no*. She really wanted to cuddle around the hearth with us and "simmer down," as she would say, after her busy day over the hot wood stove. "Did I hear you say Lay-Away Plan? It's pretty late to go shopping now!" We loved her dignified little giggle that told us she was only kidding.

Dad nudged the protruding end of the glowing log back into its iron grate. He knew we were awake because we slapped with glee at the shooting sparks that landed on the rag rug that we had helped Mom stitch together.

"I see that I am going to have to hurry, boys, or your mother will hide the cookie jar!" Dad slid his arm around her slender waist which meant: I love you, especially when you don't interrupt. "Now listen close. *God* put the heat in that log! But it wasn't easy. First He had to devise (that means, put together) His Lay-Away Plan. It had to be perfect, right from the start, so that all things would work out right on schedule as He created them. He was preparing everything *before* He made us.

"God knew that He could never die, and that meant that anything He made could last forever. He knew that everything which He would ever make would come *out of Him, even logs*! Sounds funny, doesn't it? But *He was all there was*, anywhere! And besides, being the Eternal God He also knew that everything He would make had to start out perfect, just like Himself. If any one misused something, He would have His Repair Plan ready to use on a moment's notice. As He created, He made everything we would need.

He saw that all things must someday end up like a completed puzzle with all the parts fitting perfectly. Our Creator made *preparations* for an abundant life and for everything that we would need in His universe. He showed us how to make things to turn out right, so we could use His plan as our example. Jesus said, "Follow Me, I am the Way... ."

"It's time for bed now, and you may wonder why I told you such a strange true story tonight. You'll understand better tomorrow when I tell you about the most amazing part of the Lay-Away Plan. It will explain why there is a Christmas. In fact I will give you a clue to sleep on.

### A Clue and A Surprise

"When God was putting His plan together for all creation He was shocked to see one of the most important pieces out of place. It was down near the end of the Plan. It was to be one of His last creations, and was meant to be very special. He looked closely, and saw that it was labeled *World*. In amazement He looked very closely again, and His heart sank at what He saw.

"Frightened people that looked like lost sheep were running aimlessly all over His World. He could see them falling down before idols. They were being driven wild by hordes of nasty-looking fallen angels who told them lies. They were lost and didn't know where they were, and it scared them to death!

### The Father's Revised Preparation

"God turned back to His blueprint and added a notation; it said something like this:

"When the time is right, I will send down to the World a perfect BOY-LAMB so that those lost sheep will hear His voice and get to know Him. He will be called JESUS, the SAVIOR. He will be born in a manger like a little lamb; He will grow up to be their KING. He will die for them to set them free. He will be a part of Me, My Only Begotten Son!"

The clock bonged. "My goodness, boys, it's nearly Christmas! Here's a kiss. I'll be up to tuck you in."

# Chapter 2

# The Creation

*In the beginning God created the heaven and the earth.*

Genesis 1:1 KJV

*These things saith the Amen, the faithful and true witness, the beginning of the creation of God.* Revelation 3:14b KJV

*For by Him all things were created: things in heaven and on earth, visible and invisible, whether thrones or powers or rulers or authorities; all things were created by Him and for Him.*

Colossians 1:16

*And forgettest [thou] the Lord thy maker, that hath stretched forth the heavens, and laid the foundations of the earth...?*

Isaiah 51:13 KJV

# Christmas Came, Right on Time

**B**rother tried to sneak out of our bedroom in the morning without waking me. But it didn't work. It was still dark enough that he tripped over a shoe he had left in the doorway. By the time he had slid down the stairs and bumped every banister, Dad and Mom were standing in their doorway too.

We knew that he was fighting back the tears from his injured "dignity." (Dad called it that whenever we were not really hurt.) "But, Mom, I didn't mean to wake you, really I didn't!"

Their laughter soothed the pain. "MERRY CHRIST-MAS! We thought it was Santa Claus falling down the chimney. Lucky it was only you! Just think of all the soot he would have gotten on his red flannels!" (I was thinking more about the blisters he would have gotten from the hot coals, and whether butter or Dr. Peer's Golden Medical Discovery was best for burns.)

Brother was already around the pot-bellied stove and headed for the red stockings thumb-tacked to the mantel. By the time we got downstairs, I heard his shout of glee, and knew that any bruises were forgotten. Sure enough, Santa had been there already. Dad and Mom had seen to that! Their Lay-Away Plan had been work-ing in secret. They remained at the doorway, looking through the strings of hanging wooden beads that let the warmth from the fireplace filter out into the dining room. It was obvious that for some reason their *real* Christmas joy was in watching *us*!

Bob and I found the usual things in the feet of our socks. Each Christmas since the "WAR" had ended we had reached down and pulled out a real orange and two walnuts! They had been sent clear from California by "little old, Grandma," from her trees—picked 'specially for us. They meant, "I love you." They would be the only oranges and walnuts we would see all year. Grandma knew that we would cherish looking at them, until Mom would say one fateful morning, "Boys, you'd better eat your presents before they turn bad!"

And sure enough, there were the two pencils and gum rubber erasers that we needed for our drawing books. What a wonderful Christmas! We ran and hugged Dad and Mom; they were the best parents. After all, we had heard of children who didn't have any parents at all.

### Christmas—A Holy-day

Dad had told us that Christmas was a holiday. That meant a special day. He explained that it was really a *Holy-day*. That meant two things: it was a day to honor God who is Holy, and a day of rest from the usual jobs that people have to do. In the old days, he told us, the Holy-days were meant to be "family days" when the grown-ups and kids could have a whole day together to get better acquainted. They also were expected to learn something more about God during that day. He said that God had made us to worship Him every day, but especially on Holy-days. It would be time "well spent" (one of Dad's favorite words).

Christmas mornings always went too fast. Mother was already rinsing the luncheon dishes in the steaming water-well in the end of the iron range. Dad's leather rocking chair with the walnut arms was groaning to the rhythm of his steady pushes; he was proudly admiring his new box of shells with their "rabbit" loads. Next Saturday he would try out a couple in the woodlot behind the barn. He was a happy man, we could tell, as we "surrounded" him, one on each side.

"Dad," I queried, "You said once that God made us to worship Him. Did you mean that He really made you and me? And everybody? How come kids have parents, and grandparents, if God makes us?"

The armchair stopped squeaking, and Dad laid his shell box carefully aside. "That's a good question, Richard. I did say that God made us. It is all part of that Lay-Away Plan of His. You'll remember that I told you last night how God's Plan is like a great puzzle with so many pieces that He lays some of them away until He is ready to use them. Each piece has to fit, one after the other." We nodded.

### In the Beginning—Only God

"You see, in the beginning God created the heavens and the earth. No one else was around to give advice. There was no one else who knew how. So He started out by making a great Plan. We do not know how long He took thinking about all the suns and stars and gases and lights and trees and animals and foods it would take to make His Plan work. We just know that He was too smart to start creating until He knew that all the pieces of His great puzzle would fit together perfectly.

"Some of the pieces would not be needed right away. He would use them later on. He probably put them aside with His blueprint in a file called: *Planet Earth—Special Details.* In small print He added: *Hold Till Needed.*

"I can imagine that there was another file next to the first one, probably gold with red borders, labeled *LOVE AFFAIR.* There were pages labeled "My Lamb," "His Lambs," "Our Family," and "Plans for Our New Home." Each page had required endless amounts of planning!

"I told you about the *amazing* part last night, the story about God preparing a Lamb to die for people's needs long before there were any people! There wasn't even an earth yet! God's plan was to make a universe full of heavens and stars and worlds for Him to enjoy, something like a huge playground. Then He would make angels to live with Him and work for Him—millions and millions of them. They would be so happy to be with Him because they could always be praising the Lamb!

"Are they still there?" Bob interrupted. Dad patted my brother's shoulder. "Some of them are! The night when you died of pneumonia four years ago I had asked God to send your guardian angel to watch over you while we prayed. We asked God to put His spirit back into your cold body, and He did! I have often wondered what your angel said to God that night: probably, 'Do it, God, or I will be out of business.' Well, your angel is still awfully busy with you on some days!" I saw his arm tighten around Bob in a big hug.

"Better pull up those cushions and sit down, boys. The exciting part is next.

"One day, we're told, God's Creation Plan was completed. Everything was in orderly fashion. He could see from the beginning to the end of what He called "eternity"; and what He saw would all fit together as He had wished.

### Another Great Idea—The Three-in-One God

"Then God realized that the job of making a huge universe was too big for the mind of man ever to understand because man would *first* have to understand God and how He works! After much thought He decided to divide Himself into three pieces or parts (we call them *Persons*). Each Person would have certain jobs assigned to Him, although each One could do any of them. This would make it easier! One Person would be the Father, one the Son, and one the Holy Spirit. Does that make it easier to understand?"

Both Bob and I frowned. It sounded simple, but could Dad give us a "for instance," we asked. "Come here, Mother, please. Thank you, Dear. How would you like to be an illustration of God? For you it will come natural!" They beamed at each other, and she wrinkled her nose at him.

"Now, boys, who is standing in front of you?"

"Mom, of course!" we quickly answered.

"But she's not my mom," Dad reminded us.

"No, she is your wife!"

"Right! And she is Grandma's daughter as well. That makes her a mother, a wife, and a daughter—all at the same time; but she is one woman, one fine lady, I might add! Think again: She loves you with her sweet spirit, and she teaches you with her good mind, and she hugs you to her warm body when you are cold. She is a spirit, mind, and body—but she is still only one person! Catch on?"

We nodded. (It must be part of God's Plan to make things simple for kids to understand. At least He sent them teachers like Dad with lots of brains, but with simple ways of explaining hard things.)

"Surprise, surprise!" Mother's cheery voice rang from the kitchen as she emerged with our favorite snack, blueberry muffins hot from the oven. Ummh, were they good! Even though it meant brushing our teeth an extra time today, it was worth it. Last July we had climbed Berry Mountain where the old stagecoach road used to climb over the Berkshire Hills on its way to Boston. We had loaded two buckets with berries—fat, blue, and juicy—and now Mom was "rewarding her men" with a feast. She must have forgiven us for coming home that day with blue stains all over our pants and blouses! I could remember her reddened knuckles when she had finished rinsing the blue Fels Naptha suds from the scrub board that night.

We had had a quiet nap and a light Christmas supper before we decided to ask Dad about the story which the muffins had interrupted. (Story-telling started when the sun went down and we couldn't see well enough to read picture books or to do coloring.) Besides, it was popcorn time around the fireplace. And the eight chimes from the clock in the living room told us that only four hours were left in this Christmas day.

"Thanks, Dad, for a wonderful Christmas," I announced. "I liked the story you told, but what happened after God finished His Plan? Did it work?"

### The Plan That Worked

He fished the last of the kernels out of their milky bath, drained his bowl dry of the buttery milk, and reached for his old worn Bible. He couldn't read it in the dark, but he loved to hold it as he talked. He said that it and he had been through some hard times together. He said its words were an "ever constant source of comfort" (whatever that meant). He knew it worked that way for him.

"Richard, it worked! The reason we can know that His Plan worked is found in the Bible. You see, the Holy Spirit could tell wise men what to write, because the Spirit of God had watched Him make everything. God simply *thought* what He wanted to make, and there it was! Sometimes He *spoke*, and there it was! Sometimes He pointed, and a star stopped in its tracks and just hung there. He called for a sun and then a moon, and there they were!"

"That must have been fun for God," Bob added.

"Not fun enough," Dad explained. "The Bible tells us that after God created the universe, He let it set for a long, long time. His Plan called for oil and gases and minerals that form from dying forests and animals and fishes. It took millions of years for that part of His Plan to be prepared for the next part—the exciting part!"

Just then Mom filled his bowl with more popcorn, and he stopped to "sample" it.

### The Villain and the Victor

"Let's back up a minute while you chew a few mouthfuls. Ready? There's a villain in this story. All the time that God was busy making the good things every where, His most powerful angel, called Lucifer, was scheming to destroy them. Lucifer was *so jealous* that he decided to replace God, and sit on His throne! God was rightfully angry, so angry that He threw lucifer out of Heaven, and changed his name to *satan*. Satan was so angry that he decided to ruin God's beautiful World. And he did. It became a chaos (that means, a total mess)!

"God sat back for a long time; then He said to His Holy Spirit: 'Go down there and move back and forth and separate the mud back into water and land. I am going to have My Son, My Lamb, remake things beautiful again, like a garden, so I can walk there!' "

"Was that the exciting part of His plan?" I blurted out.

"Not yet! It was exciting enough, though. Just imagine all the fishes and birds and other animals suddenly being made in just the *right* numbers and places to find the *right* foods already waiting for their dinners! That took planning, for sure. Then the BIG DAY came!"

### "Let Us Make Man"

Our eyes widened in wonder. "Yes, God wanted someone to love, someone like Him! He said to His Son and to His Spirit: 'Let's make a man like Us. Son, You be his Creator. Spirit, You become his Breath. This is the moment I planned! Make his body out of mud, blow on him, and he will be a living soul. Try it. You'll see that he is very, very good!' "

The room seemed so quiet all at once. Our little minds were working over this amazing story while Dad let it "soak in." Could it be true that we were made of mud? Beyond that, did that *great* God make us because He loved *our* company? How could He love *us* and want *us* around Him? We weren't smart enough yet even to talk with God. Besides, if we kids played hide-and-go-seek with Him, He would always win 'cause He could find us anywhere; it wouldn't be fair. Well, maybe it would be; 'cause when He found us He would probably give *us* a good present for being His friend. It would be fun to find out.

Mom spoke up: "Past your bedtime, boys! Thank you for those beautiful clothespins, so smooth and clean! It was a lovely Christmas, wasn't it? All of us together again. Let's hold hands and thank God for being so good!" Her hands were so gentle, and Dad's were firm.

There was nothing to fear that night. Somehow we knew we were a part of His Plan. Even though God had waited so long to put us boys on earth, we felt even more important because He had been planning for us to live when His puzzle was almost completed! Perhaps we would get to see the end of His PLAN.

# Chapter 3

# The Judgment

*For this one man, Adam, brought death to many through his sin. But this one man, Jesus Christ, brought forgiveness to many through God's mercy. Adam's one sin brought the penalty of death to many, while Christ freely takes away many sins and gives glorious life instead.*
Romans 5:15-16 TLB

*...in Adam all die...*
1 Corinthians 15:22

*But you must not eat from the tree of the knowledge of good and evil, for when you eat of it you will surely die.*
Genesis 2:17

*To Adam He said, "Because you listened to your wife and ate from the tree about which I commanded you, 'You must not eat of it, Cursed is the ground because of you; through painful toil you wil eat of it all the days of your life. It will produce thorns and thistles fo you...until you return to the ground, since from it you were taken; fo dust you are and to dust you will return. "*
Genesis 3:17-19

# Sheepskins and Lambskins

Wintertime was fun for us boys. Pontoosuc Lake became a sheet of glass dotted with sheepskin coats on weekends. The sounds of ice chisels echoed toward the shores. Excited fishermen cut holes and set their "tip-ups" with the little red flags. Children's screams of delight added to the chilly sounds whenever a flag flew upright at the tug of a fat perch on the line.

All the children wore skates, the clamp-on kind. We laughed at each other's wobbling ankles as we challenged the girls to keep from falling down less often than us boys. Then we would hide among the "ice castles" along the stony shore where the wind had piled up huge chunks. Between them was drifted snow, just right for the daily "snow fights" between the Injuns and the Rebels.

One thing brought us back to reality: our mothers' calls from shore—"Hot cocoa!" Nothing else mattered when cocoa was ready! Even the men in sheepskin coats stopped their chiseling and joined our flight toward the steaming drums over the coals. Tomorrow would be Sunday School and dress-up clothes, but today it didn't matter if we got cocoa and fish scales on our "throw-away" pants. Mother said they couldn't last through the winter anyway. Besides, brown spots and fishy smells meant that we were having fun with Dad, and getting some fish too!

## To School On Sunday

Although brother and I were not the same age, we were the same size, so we went into the same Sunday School class. He called me a runt. I said: "That's OK; if you're so big, you can help me poke anybody in the nose who tries to fight me!" Of course, I knew he would anyway; he would even cry when Dad had to spank *me*! I guessed that was what brothers were for, just being around to help out.

When Mr. Basset, our teacher on Sundays, would ask a question, it was an unspoken contest to see which of us would answer first. The lesson today was about Adam, the *first man to walk with God*. Mr. Basset said it must have been exciting for both of them: Adam needed someone to show him around, and God for the first time had someone on earth to talk to! God said, "Please name everything you see anywhere!" And Adam did it, right off the bat, because he had a brand-fresh mind that worked much like God's.

Mr. Basset said that God was delighted! "Adam," He said, "you can do anything in the whole world now, except one thing. Don't eat the pretty fruit on that one tree over there in the middle of My garden. Don't even touch that tree. It belongs to Me alone. If you do, you will surely die!" (Bob and I looked at each other. We knew what God had meant. It was just like Dad had told us about that one special row of corn he planted behind the cottage last spring. "Boys," he had warned us, "that is what's called *hybrid* corn—very special— sixteen rows of kernels to the cob. I am one of the first to receive a test packet. This will be *my* row. *Leave it alone* so I can be responsible for anything good or bad that comes from my experiment." We obeyed, for sure!)

"It was the tree of knowledge about right and wrong," explained Basset. "Do any of you know what happened next?"

### The Fatal Mistake—Disobedience

Both our hands flew up. He pointed to me. "Yes, Mister. Adam told his wife, Eve, what God had said. But he didn't know that a beautiful-looking serpent had been lying to her already. The snake told Eve she was almost as smart as God so she might as well get smarter. He said that *God* was a liar. He said the fruit was already ripe and should be eaten; it couldn't hurt her at all. Besides it was delicious, and would make her smarter than God!"

"What did she do about satan's temptation, Richard?"

"Well, she sneaked over to that tree when Adam was away fishin' or somethin' and ate a bite. It tasted so good that she gave a piece to Adam that evening when he came home late. Just then the moon came up and they could see each other."

Robert giggled and poked me: "Tell them what they saw."

I had to answer. "They were, were, nay-ked! And they ran away and hid in the dark. They were so scared that God would see them. He had said they would surely die. That made them more scared, so they hid behind some big green leaves!"

By now the whole class was giggling. But Mr. Basset saved the day. "Children, you were born that way—naked all over! Do you know what your mother or dad did right away? Of course you do; they put clothes on you. That was part of *their* plan for you before you arrived. They had prepared in advance. *So had God!*"

This time little Marion got her hand up first: "How did God plan to put clothes on them anyhow?" she asked between shrugs.

Bob turned to Marion: "Just ask *me*! He had a Lay-Away Plan to take care of anything that could happen! My Dad said so! Don't worry. God can figure out those kinds of things!" Bob felt he had scored a point, for sure. (Mr. Basset was smiling over a little phrase that went through his head—"...out of the mouths of babes.")

He cleared his throat. "That's about right, Robert. I had not thought of it that way before. The Bible tells us that God did not want anyone to die from exposure to heat or cold or even sin (that's *disobedience*). People were always meant to be His most precious possessions, so He had made plans to provide them with different kinds of clothing. Right?"

All the youngsters nodded agreement. "What do you suppose He planned to use against sin?" No heads moved this time. "This will surprise you: He chose a Lamb! It was to be a Boy-Lamb with several names. God said to call Him Immanuel, or Messiah, or Jesus, or Prince of Peace, or Master, or Lord, or even King! In fact your Bible gave Him hundreds of names because He was and is so special."

"Yes, but how could God use a lamb to protect us against sin?" Marion asked. "When I disobey, I don't see any lamb coming to help me?"

"Let me explain. God put the real Lamb, the Jesus-Lamb, into His Lay-Away Plan (as Robert called it). Someday *that* Lamb would be needed to protect a *worldful* of disobedient people that God calls "lost sheep" or "little lambs that went astray." That Lamb would come down to earth from Heaven and teach people not to sin anymore. But many people hated being told not to do *wrong* things which they enjoyed so much. So they killed Jesus, the Lamb of God, by tearing His skin off Him with whips, and letting Him bleed to death on a cross!"

Lois was jumping up and down with her hand raised. "Oh, I know about that! The cavalry soldiers took Jesus away from the pilot, and took a berry-bus instead!"

"Something like that, dear. You sit and listen real close now."

### The Bell Says, HURRY

Just then a faint, familiar grating sound notified us that upstairs it was nearly time for "Services." It distracted our attention from Mr. Basset for a moment. Many times we had watched the heavyset custodian of the church climb the steeple stairs at ten minutes to eleven. He would grasp the heavy manila rope that hung through a baseball-size hole in the ceiling, and give a grunt and a pull. From far above came the answering BONG from the corroded throat of the old brass bell. Back and forth swung the heavy clapper as the rope wound and unwound on the great pulley wheel with the curved spokes. When ice and snow clogged the hole, the frozen rope would catch and jump, sending shivers down the studdings clear to the basement where we sat near the hot coal furnace.

As Mr. Basset looked at his Westclox pocket watch, the little nickle gong above his head on the wall tinkled twice. We knew that meant *Hurry*—ten minutes left. He told us that God found Adam and Eve hiding. They were so ashamed to be caught red-handed in their green leaves! They needed *clothes* right away, so their Father God left and came back with two *lambskins* to wear when the sun came up. God said to them that those lambs had died to "cover" man's sins like those skin coats were *now covering man's body*. He said that their blood had been given too, so as to illustrate how it would wash away dirty sins. God explained that the *real* GOD-LAMB would cleanse their sins by shedding His own blood someday. God told them they were under JUDGMENT for their crime against Him. But He would always love them, if they would ask Him to forgive them!

The little nickle gong suddenly danced on its loose screws with a resounding ding-a-ling, just as Mr. Basset was hurrying to tell us: "Children, we'll finish next week. Just remember this: God doesn't give us everything we want the first time we meet Him. He lays away the best things for later so we can really enjoy the fun of looking ahead for them! Now run upstairs, but *quietly*. They are starting already to sing 'There Is Power In the Blood.' "

We ran down the aisle and squeezed in between Mom and Dad on the second row. It was nice and warm to snuggle between them. Besides, it would keep us from wiggling when the preacher got to using big words! We were usually lucky though; he had three children our size so he tried to talk sensibly! He said that today's "Children's Message" was about Judgment, and we better listen.

## About Sheep and Goats

"Children," he said, "you'll discover that God is very honest; He keeps His promises. He told Adam and Eve not to disobey Him or they would surely *die* and so would their children. He wasn't being mean; He was being kind and loving. He wanted them to stay *out* of trouble by avoiding something that would harm them *forever*. Someday He would have to sort all people into two groups—one would be called *sheep* [they who obeyed Him], and the others He would call *goats* [they who never did anything He told them]." (See Matthew 25:32.)

The preacher looked down at the open book on the pulpit. "You can see in the Bible how much God is like your teacher at school. Your teacher tells you what to do to get good marks, then she puts them in a Book of *Grades*. They aren't *her* grades—they are *yours*. She is your *Judge* only because she decides whether *you* followed the study rules. If you flunk, whose fault is it? Yours or hers? Let's see your hands, children. Who thinks it's *her* fault? What? No hands? Who thinks it's *your* very own fault? Well…that's…everybody!"

## God's Library of Record Books

He held up his Bible: "*This* is just *one* of God's books. God has a heavenly library. In it, we are told, there is one BOOK OF LIFE and many BOOKS OF WORKS. Everybody's name is either in one or in the others, but not in both. The single book is called the Lamb's Book of Life. God has promised that whenever you tell Him that you love Him, after your name He writes, 'I will adore this lamb forever.' And He erases *all* your faults!

"Those other books are not pleasant reading. In them God has had to write the names of people who do not love Him. They said, 'We don't want a Father in Heaven; we would rather do anything other than worship a God who says to live by *His* rules. We won't let *Him* judge what *we* should do. No sir! We'll get along by doing our *own* thing!'

"It made God very sad to write down the things they did without His permission. It took many books to record *all* their works, including their idle words! Yet it was all part of His Lay-Away Plan. He knew that someday everybody would deserve to be judged as to whether they chose to live for God or not. So God had to keep books on everybody's 'homework' to show them what they did wrong. If they 'flunked,' they could read for themselves all their mistakes. It would be *their* record—not His. (We read about the Books of Works in Revelation 20:12.)

"That's why we can call our Heavenly Father 'the *Righteous* God.' Long ago He knew that after we were born we would need a Savior to forgive our mistakes. So He prepared the Lamb (Jesus) to offer forgiveness to all children (and grown-ups too). God put the Lamb into His Lay-Away Plan because we would need Him someday—maybe right *today*!

"Now, children, I am going to talk with your parents about the wonderful way God shows His love to them. If you get a little tired, snuggle up to them, but be real quiet. They will want to hear the sermon.

"By the way, did I forget to tell you what Jesus said to the mob who hated Him for doing miracles that day? He promised them that anybody who believes on Him (that He is *really* from Heaven) *instantly* has eternal life and *shall not come under judgment* (John 5:24,29 paraphrase). He promised that believers are 'passed from death unto life.' That means that you can have all A's in *His* BOOK of LIFE if you will ask Him to be *your* teacher every day!"

# Chapter 4

# The Commandments

*Which is the first commandment of all? And Jesus answered him, The first of all the commandments is, Hear, O Israel; The Lord our God is one Lord: And thou shalt love the Lord thy God with all thy heart, and with all thy soul, and with all thy mind, and with all thy strength: this is the first commandment. And the second is like, namely this: Thou shalt love thy neighbour as thyself. There is none other commandment greater than these.*     Mark 12:28b-31 KJV

*And these words, which I command thee this day, shall be in thine heart; And thou shalt teach them diligently unto thy children, and shalt talk of them when thou sittest in thine house, and when thou walkest by the way, and when thou liest down, and when thou risest up.*     Deuteronomy 6:6-7 KJV

*And remember all the commandments of the Lord, and do them...that ye seek not after your own heart and your own eyes...That ye may remember, and do all my commandments, and be holy unto your God.*     Numbers 15:39-40 KJV

*Thy word have I hid in mine heart, that I might not sin against thee...Thou through Thy commandments hast made me wiser than mine enemies: for they are ever with me.*     Psalm 119:11,93 KJV

# Learning Means Watching and Listening

**E**ven with the best of teachers, a child's brain can only absorb so much. Children *must* grow up slowly. That has always been God's plan for them. They would always need their early years to *learn* so many things: like drinking milk, and feeling teeth grow in, and standing up instead of crawling, and learning not to touch hot stoves. There would be other things: like sitting on a potty at the right times, and getting used to little shoes that kept the gravel walkways from hurting, and learning to know words that grownups use. Growing up is especially a time for imitating big folks who go to sleep in the dark and get in the light, and only eat when the clock hands are at three different places!

For Bob and me it was, above all, a time to discover that when people got together, they seemed to pay more attention to *how* they spoke than to *what* they spoke! Sometimes we kids could tell what they meant just by how they looked. When Mom would peel potatoes and hum quietly, she didn't have to say a word; we knew supper was coming soon. She didn't have to say anything either, when she reached for the willow switch as we pulled our hands from the cookie jar! These things we learned quickly. Other *facts* came slower.

Getting information from books came slowly when we kids were first learning. Written words did not mean much. Since we could not yet spell, we didn't know what they "said" on paper. Some words sounded the same to us, but apparently meant something different. So we learned to watch where people pointed or patted when they talked, and what tone of voice they used. Mother explained that we were somewhat like the Pilgrims and Indians who could not understand each other at first. They had to use sign language, or grunt in different tones! So we tried it.

### Learning to Use Words

It was fun. The easy words were things we could point to: cuh-lock, ss-tove, wah-ter, lay-dee. The hard words were things we could not see or touch. We learned that *soft* was like a baby chickie, *sharp* was like a diaper pin, *sting* was what a bee did when we picked it up. But *love* was something else; it was being cuddled or tucked between warm blankets just out of the oven. *Patience* was waiting at mealtime till Mother took off her apron and Dad said "Thank you, Jesus" before we could start on the peanut butter and jam! We learned some other words too.

*Commandments* were something that changed the tone of people's voices when they spoke them—not angry but very firm. Usually a *commandment* was repeated with a finger pointed at us. That meant we were to obey. *Obey* meant "do it or else." The *else* could be several things, none pleasant! We got the idea that commandments were good ideas; keeping them was far more comfortable than disobeying. It was better to obey!

### Lambs Need Rules

God's commandments were made a part of His Lay-Away Plan. He discovered that the very people whom He had created to be His everlasting friends wanted to run away like dumb lambs! He had hoped that they would be like loving children to whom He could give *all* the wisdom and gifts that they could use. But right away they got into trouble; they started fighting and killing each other, and doing anything that they knew would make God unhappy.

So He wrote some rules and regulations to live by. He wrote ten of them on stone tablets. The others He dictated to scribes (secretaries) or to prophets (preachers). He told *all* parents to read them and talk about them to their children. Then He told the priests and the kings to tell other people who traveled through their towns all about these true commands for right living.

Because God loved His little lambs (they are His kids who run around His earth), He made *simple* rules for them. God always knew that it is better to *stay* out of trouble than to try to *get* out of trouble! He *knows best* how we should live each day!

He also knows that it is better to *obey* His rules than to force Him to spank us. When we do not mind Him, we get into trouble—bad trouble. If we mind Him, He gets us out of trouble, and even blesses us! His Bible tells us so:

*When you are in distress...then in later days you will return to the Lord your God and obey Him. For the Lord your God is a merciful God; He will not abandon or destroy you or forget the covenant with your forefathers, which He confirmed to them by oath...from the day God created man on the earth; ask from one end of the heavens to the other. Has anything so great as this ever happened...?*

Deuteronomy 4:30-32

There was once a very smart shepherd boy named David. His father told him to obey the rules about tending sheep. He carried a long stick with a crook on the end so he could pull frightened lambs out of holes in the rocks. He walked with them across rocky ground and led them to the greenest grass. Because he was taller than the lambs he could see ahead where the quiet pools of water had collected after the rain. Even in the scary dark canyons the lambs knew that they were safe because David was leading them.

Then one day God gave David a big surprise party. He said, "I am making you KING because you have obeyed Me!" And David suddenly realized that he had been God's little lamb-child all the time! So he sat down and wrote us about how his Lord had taken care of him:

*The Lord is my shepherd; I shall not want. He maketh me to lie down in green pastures: He leadeth me beside the still waters...I will fear no evil: for Thou art with me; Thy rod and Thy staff they comfort me.*
Psalm 23:1-2,4 KJV

## Commandments Do Not Change with the Weather

Summertime always seemed like a perfect time to change the rules! The days were longer and the clothes were lighter, and spirits were gayer. We didn't have to wear "galoshes and mittens" in order to venture forth from the cottage warmth. It seemed twice as hard to hear Mother call, "Nap time," or "Bath time," or "Chore time." In fact we would claim that she must be wrong; she was probably just *thinking* she called us. Our claims never worked though; we'd strike out every time!

Mother explained that *rules and commands* do not change for our convenience. She told me that truth while standing one day in the hot sun, hanging up wet laundry. She was already tired from working over the steaming suds in the washtub, and then cranking the hand wringer beside the hot stove. I was grumbling because little brother was down at the dock catching "punkinseeds" while *I* had to work!

She peered down at me through sweaty glasses as her reddened fingers pushed a fresh clothespin in place over my Sunday shirt. "Richard, we most often win if we play by the rules. We are *sure* to win if we follow the *Golden* Rule. Even in hot weather it works. It is really a commandment: 'Do unto others what you want them to do for you.' You like to wear clean clothes that look and smell nice when you are with your friends, don't you? So I do the laundry for you even on hot days. Don't you like someone to help you when you get tired?" (I nodded sheepishly.) "Well, so do I. If I thought it would hurt you, I wouldn't ask. Will you hand me your pillow case? It will smell sweet after drying in the sun!"

### Be a Treasure—Not a Mule

We had a homemade porch-swing that hung from the rafters. On balmy evenings we would sit next to Mom and watch the stars come out as the mountains disappeared. We would talk quietly while Dad worked on a new "invention" that had just "popped into his mind" as he drove Dickie-Whoa home from the street-car station. Mother knew that we couldn't get to sleep on these hot nights at the "regular time," so she would teach us something that we needed to know, as the stars came out.

"Richard, you may light the lamp now. I'll need to read." That meant that she trusted me with a blue-tipped match that could ignite so easily. "Now I can see…The same God that made the stars stay up in the heavens over our heads laid down some mighty important rules for us too. You have been hearing about God's Lay-Away Plan. Well, His commandments were part of that Plan. Long before you were born, or anyone in fact, He prepared rules that would work best for the people He was planning to create. Doesn't that sound smart?"

"Yeah, Mom." Bob thought a while. "I guess that is what Dad is doing upstairs. He said he had to draw his *imbention* on paper first. If it looks OK, he'll make 'em build it, and he'll get a dollar!"

Mother laughed quietly. "Yes, the same God who made your daddy made the commandments. They both work! Let me read what God says to boys about their daddies and mommies. He told the smartest man that ever lived to tell you this message. Here is what King Solomon wrote:

*My son, keep your father's commands and do not forsake your mother's teaching. Bind them upon your heart forever; fasten them around your neck. When you walk, they will guide you; when you sleep, they will watch over you; when you awake, they will speak to you. For these commands are a lamp, this teaching is a light, and the corrections of discipline are the way to life."*                    Proverbs 6:20-23

"If King Solomon were sitting here with us tonight, he would hold your hands and tell you about his father

David who was God's favorite king of all times. Solomon would be excited. He knew that God had made him wise and prosperous because he had obeyed his dad and followed the laws and commandments of the nation.

"Solomon would tell you that one day King David had told him to listen to a psalm he had just written after the Lord spoke to him:

> *I will instruct you and teach you in the way you should go; I will counsel you and watch over you. Do not be like the horse or the mule, which have no understanding..."* Psalm 32:8-9

We laughed. God sure knew about *our* horse at least! Old Dickey-Whoa still had to wear blinders so he wouldn't buck at harmless rabbits jumping across the gravel road. He had to have a bit in his mouth to tell him that Dad was still boss when he pulled on the reins! People must act like horses or mules else God wouldn't have warned David.

Mom continued: "God is disappointed when boys or grownups waste their time acting like animals. He would much rather see them obey. Before David's time, God had another favorite shepherd called Moses. This is what He told Moses one day:

> *Now if you obey Me fully and keep My covenant, then out of all nations you will be My treasured possession. Although the whole earth is Mine...* Exodus 19:5

### Obey or Perish

"Later on in history there was another man, Job, who loved God and believed another promise intended for those who obey:

> *If they obey and serve Him, they will spend the rest of their*
> *days in prosperity and their years in contentment. But if they*
> *do not listen, they will perish by the sword and die without*
> *knowledge. "*                                    Job 36:11-12

Bob was curious about these big words. "But what is *prosperity*, Mom? Do I have it?"

"Yes, Robert. In the Bible it means the opposite of disappointment. It means 'everything is going OK,' as *you* would say it. Whether we are little or big, rich or poor, God wants us to know that obedience to Him *and* to our parents will give us joy inside!"

"Well then, what does *perish* mean?"

"It can mean several things—all bad. Most of all it means that without God we dry up inside, like that shriveled cantaloupe in the garden that you accidentally didn't water last week. It dies on the vine. It goes to waste. When we disobey God intentionally, after He has given us such simple rules to live by, our spirits inside us simply wither and won't grow. *Our* God is the only source of life. Without Him we even perish *forever*, the Bible says! Jesus told His audience one day that unless they quit mocking God they would end up as though they were on the city dump where the garbage burned all the time. He said that would be terrible, like hell!"

Mom turned to reach toward the lamp. We knew by now that the story-time was over. The moonlight was breaking up into millions of silvery sparklers across the surface of the sleepy lake.

"Don't turn it out yet, please, Mom!" Bob insisted. "Will I be like garbage if I disobey God?"

She turned back and hugged him tight. "Oh, no. Part of God's Plan included you. Remember about the Lamb that His Father God provided to help little children as they grow up?" Bob nodded. "We call Him Jesus. He has already been to earth. When John the Baptist (he was the desert preacher long ago) saw Jesus on the riverbank one day he instantly recognized Him! He shouted to the people as loud as he could: '*Look*! The LAMB OF GOD who is taking away the sin of the world!'

"Jesus told the people that it was not the will of His Father who is in Heaven that one little lamb should perish! He said that Heaven was for people who are like humble children. They *trust Him* with their lives!"

This time she blew out the flame and led us to the stairway. "Sweet dreams, boys. I'll be up to tuck you in, and we'll tell Jesus how much we love Him. That was His First Commandment, wasn't it?"

# Chapter 5

# The Old Covenant

*Then God said, "Take your son, your only son, Isaac...Sacrifice him there as a burnt offering... ." Then he reached out his hand and took the knife to slay his son...Abraham looked up and there in a thicket he saw a ram [Boy-Lamb] caught by its horns...and sacrificed it as a burnt offering instead of his son...The angel of the Lord called... "I swear by Myself, declares the Lord, that because you have done this...I will surely bless you...and through your offspring [the Messiah to come] all nations on earth will be blessed, because you have obeyed Me."*         Genesis 22:2,10,13,15-18

*Was not our ancestor Abraham considered righteous for what he did when he offered his son Isaac on the altar?...And the scripture was fulfilled that says, "Abraham believed God, and it was credited to him as righteousness," and he was called God's friend.*         James 2:21,23

*Understand, then, that those who believe are children of Abraham... . If you belong to Christ, then you are Abraham's seed, and heirs according to the promise [of salvation].*         Galatians 3:7,29

*...anyone who loves his son or daughter more than Me is not worthy of Me.*         Matthew 10:37

# Learning
# Lessons
# on the Water

**T**oday was special! We were excited. It was Saturday, Dad's day off and we could go fishing for the first time since the ice had thawed. With the worms in a tin can, and some crayfish in a jar of water, we kids were *ready*! Mother had joined the fun by preparing cornmeal and seasonings for frying our catch in the heavy iron skillet. Spring days on Lake Pontoosuc were almost heavenly, and we could hardly wait.

We jumped into the round-bottom boat and Dad kicked against the dock as he hopped aboard to give us a quick start. The ripples made happy sounds against the aluminum hull. As Mom waved goodbye from the dock, we held up our hands spread wide apart to show her how big a fish each would catch. Happiness meant fishin', especially when Dad had bought a whole pound of bologna to slice for sandwiches later on Mom's warm bread! Dad grabbed the varnished oars and away we went.

It seemed that Dad could find a story worth telling in 'most anything he saw. He liked to compare things with something else to make a "good lesson," as he called it. Today was just right for a few minutes of "comparisons" as he pulled on the long oak oars.

One example, he said, was our boat. It was like *hope*; it was designed to keep us afloat on the "sea of life" if we followed the rules! The heavy stone we would use as an anchor was like *firm faith*; it was to keep us from drifting aimlessly. Even the oars could be likened to *good intentions*; they were useless unless put to work. As for *fishing*, it was like our *belief* in God's love for us; for best results we must not hurry! Just enjoy every minute that He gives us, be quiet and await His instructions while He is teaching us to fish His way, and then get busy and work hard when He says *now*!

As he headed the boat toward the south end of an island, Dad explained that Jesus once said He had come to make "fishers of men" mostly out of fishermen! The reason might be that sometimes the rewards of fishing are big catches, and sometimes just small ones, but the fun is in *going* fishing! Besides, the real reward, he said, comes from sharing the *catch* with others. Dad said that someday we would better understand how exciting it is to share what Jesus can do for "poor fish in the sea of life" when they get on His "lifeline."

The oars bit into the clear water, and we slowed to a stop. The day was just right. Lazy thin clouds. Occasional whiffs of apple blossoms from the old trees on Indian Island. We anchored near the bed of pond lilies. Spreading ringlets appeared here and there as the feeding perch inhaled floating mayflies before their wings could expand. I noted spring leaves and bugs and budding flowers for my scrapbooks. (Little did I know that sixty years later my box of "pressed specimens" would be prized by our grandchildren in the city where wild flowers couldn't grow!)

I leaned over the edge of the boat to squint down through the crystal clear water. It was soon obvious that I knew too little about how God worked. Somehow the water was holding the boat on top of it, like a solid. Yet I could put my hand into it and it wasn't solid. I could see the clouds reflected in it like a mirror, and at the same time look way down to the mossy rocks on the bottom, like it was only air. I saw a skinny little pickerel dart under the boat and then hang motionless in the shadows. How could it do *that* without sinking?

It seemed quite natural to ask Dad some questions about God's reasons for doing so many nice things. Now that our lines were rigged with worms and corks, and floating (somehow?) on the water, this would be a good time to learn something!

I looked at Dad seated between his tackle box and our paper bag of bologna and buns: "Last winter," I began, "Mr. Basset told us about a man named Abraham whom God loved so very much. He said Abraham loved God too; but he never had a boy of his own. So, God promised him one even though he was nearly a hundred years old. Wow, I'll bet he and his wife were surprised when Isaac arrived! But I have a question: Why did God tell Abraham, after his son grew up, to take him for a walk up the mountain and kill him?"

There was no answer right away, so I continued: "Was that true? Suppose God asked you to do that to me, Dad! I know *you* wouldn't!"

He continued to squint at his cork as it rode the ripples. (I had not realized that I was really asking him to decide between loving God and loving me.) Then he reached forward over the tackle box and grasped my shoulder tenderly.

"I could never answer that question, Richard, unless I knew the rest of the story. You see, I love you just loads, and so does God. He made you, and I just help to raise you. The answer is this: *I* don't have to make that choice! It is all taken care of in the COVENANT that Mr. Basset told you about. That was an agreement that God made with Abraham and all the human race, *if* they would be *obedient*. He said He would provide a Lamb in Isaac's place. Do you remember what happened that day to prove that God keeps His promises?"

"Sure." Bob tried to interrupt, so I hurried my answer. "Abraham heard a noise; he turned around; he saw a lamb in some bushes; he untied Isaac and tied the lamb in his place and killed the lamb instead."

Dad was grinning ear to ear: "I think you just said a mouthful! Isn't that what boys say when they 'tell it all'? Mr. Basset must be a good teacher. You already know more than some members of my 'Y' Bible Class!

"That lamb was like a little illustration of God's Lamb (who was really God's beloved Son to be born hundreds of years later). God's Lamb died in our place so no Dad would have to kill his own dear son to prove he loved God! God has already substituted *His* only Son! That shows how much God really loved the people in His world. God never asks anybody nowadays to kill lambs. Instead, He now asks people to *thank* Him for sending His God-Lamb!"

I frowned. "Didn't the men at the 'Y' understand that? You made it real simple for me, Dad. Are grown-ups hard to teach?" He nodded. "Sometimes. They are not always sure that God would love them that much. Although Jesus, the Lamb, paid *all* the costs of saving everybody from the punishment for their wrongdoings, some people just won't believe it, since nobody else ever did that for anybody. Most grownups want to do *works* to get *all* the glory for themselves!"

"Does that idea ever work? Can we ever wash away *our own* sins like the Bible says Jesus came to do?" Bob asked.

"Not according to God's Bible, Son. That is our textbook. It says that everybody has 'come short of the *glory* of God.' That means that when anybody wants to *buy* his own salvation, he simply doesn't have enough change, no matter how many pocketsful he has! By the way, did Mr. Basset tell you any more about the Covenant God gave Abraham and his descendants—so they wouldn't be shortchanged—*not ever*?"

"He said something about... ." Just then two corks disappeared from the surface and began racing along under the ripples. Through the clear water we could see flashes of gold and silver fins heading for the pickerel weeds on the bottom. The cane poles bent over as though trying to point at our perch, the first of the season. Dad and Bob exchanged instructions about "keep the line taut," "don't pull the hook out," "watch out for the anchor rope," "It's a whopper!"

For the next few minutes we were too busy catching fat perch to learn more about the Covenant. Bob and I were so excited over watching the fish flopping around Dad's feet that we even forgot about our favorite bologna sandwiches that he had must made. We knew that he would finish the story of the Covenant later. Right now we were catching a favorite meal for Mother whose faith had led her to grease the iron skillet even before we had left the dock.

### We Learn About the Old Covenant

Four months later a swarm of city people descended on the Lake. Red canoes and while sailboats joined the wrinkled, colored leaves that skittered over the water ahead of the gusty breeze. Yesterday's newspaper had carried a headline: FINE WEATHER FOR LABOR DAY. Today was it!

Out of the many buggies and fancy opentop Lizzies and Reo's that parked along the dirt road behind our cottage poured dozens of "city kids" in short pants and high spirits.

Four of the bigger boys split off. They returned to the daisy field behind our garden, each carrying a flat rock from the stone wall across the gravel road. "Put home plate here," yelled the leader. "Carl, put your stone opposite me over *there* and you two other fellows put first and third over *there*, and *there*!" It surely sounded official. Bob and I watched in wonder.

Again the leader yelled and waved: "Come over here!" Like trained hunting dogs the boys clustered around him. "Let's choose up sides. Carl, you pick a boy, then I'll take one, till everybody is on a team. Let's go!"

We didn't see a signal, but all at once half the boys spread out around the field. The others huddled beside our toolshed and started grabbing hands, all the time shouting, "Rah, rah, team!"

"What are these city kids doing anyway?" Bob whispered in my ear. I shrugged. We hadn't seen so many boys in one place, ever. Whatever they had in mind, it must be fun. They acted like rabbits let out of the bag, running and jumping when somebody threw a round ball at them. Just then a chubby boy swung his thick club and hit the ball nearly to the horse barn, way past the farthest stone. Someone's dad with a blue cap on his head yelled "Home Run," and the boys by the toolshed behind our house jumped up and down and slapped each other's hands again.

At twilight the buggies and cars pulled away and we suddenly felt hungry. At supper Dad explained that it was called *Baseball*. He at one time had been the "pitcher" on his college team out in Colorado. "They said I won quite a few games for them," he admitted, "but I really didn't. *Everybody* on the team either wins or loses when they play. It's called 'a team effort'. That's why the boys clasped hands before they played; it was like they were all brothers during the game!"

He took a bite of our favorite brown bread made with real molasses. "That reminds me. I never finished telling you about that Abraham Covenant. It will help me to explain what you watched today. Baseball is like a covenant; the boys all agree to do their best, and they promise to share the victory!"

It took us quite a while to finish supper while Dad told us the story of the Old Covenant that God made with men. It was important that all people should know it so they could tell others as they grew up. He said that even children would enjoy life better if they learned at an early age how much God loved them. Even *before* He let them be born, *He* had loved them. The Bible said so. The proof was His Covenant!

## We Learn About the Blood Covenant

He explained that a covenant is a solemn agreement between boys or grownups or countries, or between God and the people He created. In the ancient times when there were no papers and pencils to write things down, a covenant was made by cutting a little place on the wrists of two people and catching their drops of blood in a little cup. As their friends watched, they mixed the blood drops around in the cup, and announced that they were "blood brothers." Then they rubbed some dirt into the cuts to make a good scar to show everyone else that each had a *real* blood brother!

The exciting part was *what* they said. They promised to share their wealth and their food. They would fight for each other's honor. They would even die for each other! They ended their ceremony by swapping their coats, their shoes, and their weapons. This meant that each one would walk in the other's *shoes*, be covered with the other's *coat*, and fight with the other's *sword*. They would always *share* everything!

"Those boys today didn't know that they were acting out an ancient ritual to help each other win," he added. "Now do you understand better what is meant by a blood covenant?"

"Yes, but what's that got to do with Abraham and us?" I asked. "Did God or Abraham cut their wrists?"

"No, Son, God had a *better* Plan. He made an agreement with the first man, and all the people after him. He promised to forgive them if they would have faith in Him that He would someday send a Messiah to save them forever. The Messiah would be a perfect Lamb who would shed all His blood, and have scars on *both* His wrists *and* His side, *and* His feet too!

"But in the meantime, He commanded those who had faith to prove it! They would use an animal, a healthy *lamb* if they had one, and shed its blood instead of their own. (Then for a scar to show that they were blood brothers with God, He told them to be circumcised as babies.) He said *His* Lamb would someday come as a *baby* in a manger."

A couple of tears fell onto Dad's plate. He swallowed hard. "Children, can you realize what God was promising? He would let His perfect Lamb, *His own Son*, be a blood brother for all the people-lambs, although He knew in advance that *His* Lamb would have to *die* for them!"

There was silence for quite a while. We never had seen our Dad cry, even when he was once hurt painfully with a piece of nail in his eye. He was the bravest man we knew. His tears must mean much; more than we could guess.

"Sorry, boys, but those were tears of *joy*! I can't help being so thankful that I have a God who takes care of you and Mother. When I am gone from home, I still know that you are safe. It is because of that Covenant. God *has* to keep His promises—especially now."

I interrupted while he wiped his nose. "Why did you say 'especially now,' Dad?"

"I think you can guess the answer already, but I will give the clue from the Bible. The Lord Jesus tried to explain to some angry people at the Temple just why He had come from Heaven. He said, 'I have come to *fulfill* the *law* and the *prophets*!' He meant that the promised Lamb was already on earth, standing right in front of them! They *should* have known their Covenant by heart; and that when He made His new Covenant with them the Old Covenant would not be needed anymore. You boys nowadays can know for sure that Jesus already *did die* for you two thousand years ago! Then He arose to make sure that the New Covenant would work out just right!"

Mother was wiping her hands on the dishtowel as she bent over Dad. She whispered so we could hear: "Eugene, the boys promised to pick up their coloring books before bedtime. Maybe they should get started now?"

"Of course, Mother. I had such a good audience that I kept them listening. Now boys, let's leave the front room nice and neat for tomorrow! Leave a note under my plate when you get ready to talk about the *New* Covenant. It is even more exciting... ."

# Chapter 6

# The New Covenant

*After the same manner also He took the cup...saying, This cup is the new testament in My blood: this do ye, as oft as ye drink it, in remembrance of Me. For as often as ye eat this bread, and drink this cup, ye do shew the Lord's death till He come.*

1 Corinthians 11:25-26 KJV

*Behold the Lamb of God...*                         John 1:29b KJV

*...ye were not redeemed with corruptible things...but with the precious blood of Christ, as of a Lamb without blemish and without spot...the Lamb slain from the foundation of the world.*

1 Peter 1:18-19; Revelation 13:8 KJV

*"The time is coming," declares the Lord, "when I will make a new covenant with the house of Israel and with the house of Judah."*

Jeremiah 31:31

*...a new covenant—not of the letter but of the Spirit; for the letter kills, but the Spirit gives life.*                    2 Corinthians 3:6

*May the God of peace, who through the blood of the eternal covenant brought back from the dead our Lord Jesus, that great Shepherd of the sheep, equip you with everything good for doing His will, and may He work in us what is pleasing to Him, through Jesus Christ, to whom be glory for ever and ever. Amen.*

Hebrews 13:20-21

# A Time for Thanksgiving

**S**ooner than expected, the ten pumpkins between the dried-up cornstalks out back were ready for storing in the hayloft. Thanksgiving excitement was in the air. Mother laid out our heavy woolen socks along with the lined knickers. Overhead we watched V-formations of honking geese headed south. Flights of hungry grosbeaks stripped the chokecherry hedges of their last berries.

Indian summer was over and like the chipmunks in our old stone wall we were ready to hole in for the winter.

Hardly had all the leaves fallen when one morning we smelled that yummy aroma of bread and bacon stuffin' simmering on the stove overnight. We always had a goose for Thanksgiving dinner. Mother said a goose was just the right size for her enamel roaster. But when I asked Dad if we could have a turkey this year, he said he could get a goose for half as much money as a turkey! "We won't tell Mother," he added, "but we'll save the extra money toward her Christmas present. She needs a coat without holes in it this winter!" He winked at me, and that sealed our secret. Who needed turkey anyway?

### This was a "Q & A Day"

One thing I did on Sundays and special days (now that I could write) was to slip little notes under Dad's and Mom's plates at dinnertime. Each would contain a question that I wanted answered after we had finished our desert. Bob would whisper his question in my ear so I could write it for him. He always giggled softly as he hid it under a plate.

Dad wiped his mouth and finished his cider. "Can I look now, Richard?" He read my scrawled question: "What...is...the...new...covanunt?"

He looked up at Mother and smiled. "Dear, we were discussing the Old Covenant with the boys last spring when that big school of perch came by. I told them to ask me about the New One when they got ready. It is a great Thanksgiving subject!" (I was glad he was my Dad. No matter how dumb some of my questions must have been, he always said that they were especially good, and needed to be asked! He always answered so I would understand.)

### New Is Better Than Old

"You may not understand all that I will try to tell you, but I'll make it simple. God's thoughts are bigger than ours, but when we love Him and study the Holy Bible, He helps us to know what He means. He wouldn't have given us a Bible at all if we couldn't ever learn from it, would He? Someday you will find that it contains answers to every question about how God thinks and works!

"It certainly has the answer about the *New* Covenant. Do you remember God's Plan to send a holy Lamb someday to die *once* to wash away men's sins? When that finally happened, the *New* Covenant started between God and man. Almost two thousand years ago the Lamb (Jewish people call Him the Messiah in the Old Covenant) came as the Christ-child. He gave us the *New* Covenant to improve on the old one.... .

"The new one was *much* better; it was based on *love* instead of *law*. It said that loving one another fulfilled those harsh commandments that Abraham gave the people.

"I want to read one of my favorite scriptures to you. It may sound rather 'churchy' to you, but I want you to know that it is in the Bible. If you read it slowly someday you will be excited about this New Covenant; yes, here it is:

> *But the ministry Jesus has received is as superior to theirs as the covenant of which He is mediator is superior to the old one, and it is founded on better promises. For if there had been nothing wrong with that first covenant, no place would have been sought for another...When Christ came as high priest of the good things that are already here...He entered the Most Holy Place once for all by His own blood, having obtained eternal redemption...for this reason Christ is the mediator of a new covenant...* " Hebrews 8:6-7; 9:11-12,15

Dad could see my frown as I tried to understand some of those big Bible words! What was a *mediator*? I only knew that a meteor was a bright light in the sky... *was Jesus a kind of star?*

"Yes, in a way," Dad explained. "Our Mediator is something like a meteor! Jesus is our Mediator, because He stands between us and Heaven so He can tell our Heavenly Father what we need to know. Besides, Jesus is the Light of Heaven; He lets us be His little reflectors! There is one big difference though; Jesus' light never goes out. Only once, on the cross, when He became our sin-bearer, He had to let His light die out for a while to *ransom* us.

> *For there is one God, and one mediator between God and men, the man Christ Jesus, who gave Himself a ransom for all..."*        1 Timothy 2:5-6 KJV

## Intermission Time

Mother had noticed that there was just enough pumpkin pie left in the tin to divide into three "slivers." Slyly she slipped them in front of us to give a "break" before Dad would finish his story. Whenever there was no piece left for her, we would always hear her explain that she had to "watch her figure." Dad would always reply, "That's my job; it looks fine!" Then we'd all laugh as we watched her slender frame at work over the dishes. She was certainly the prettiest lady we knew!

"Well, boys, you may wish that you had asked me for a shorter answer. But someday I won't be around to tell you these things. Other people will be asking *you* instead!" Dad reached over and patted our heads, and I took the dishes to the sink.

## How the New Covenant Works

"One final fact about this New Covenant you must know; it is for *everybody*. In the ancient days God chose special people to tell the world about Him. They were called Jews or Israelites. With them He talked and walked and made covenants. Later Jesus came down from Heaven. He told us that all men were equally in need of God's love and salvation. They *all* could *now* enjoy His promises although He once gave them to the Israelites only. Let us read these verses:

*"The time is coming,"* declares the Lord, *"when I will make a new covenant with the house of Israel and with the house of Judah...after that time,"* declares the Lord. *"I will put My law in their minds and write it on their hearts. I will be their God, and they will be My people...I will forgive their wickedness and will remember their sins no more."*

Jeremiah 31:31,33,34

"This means that God will talk *directly* to His chosen children (those who are listening) just as though His words were being written on their hearts! Everybody who obeys Him will be His people! We now can pray in Jesus' Name *directly* to Father God in Heaven, because we are His children, His little lambs. Jesus' blood has *sealed* the New Covenant with us, and our Father in Heaven calls us 'His family.'

"Isn't that simple for children to understand now? We don't have to kill a lamb to get God's attention. We aren't saved by the hundreds of laws that were included in the old agreement. God knew that we couldn't do them right anyway."

### The Covenant Is To Be Obeyed

Dad stopped a while, then scowled. He seemed suddenly sad. "Boys, our God is also a *just* God! When someone breaks a covenant, He serves also as a just *Judge*. Like a good Father, He *must* punish lawbreakers. When people ridicule His Son Jesus for dying in their place, God's Word says, 'Watch Out.' "

*How much more severely do you think a man deserves to be punished who has trampled the Son of God under foot, who has treated as an unholy thing the blood of the covenant that sanctified him, and who has insulted the Spirit of grace?*

Hebrews 10:29

"Tell your little friends to love Jesus and obey His rules; then everything turns out OK! God said so."

*But I gave them this command: Obey Me, and I will be your God and you will be My people. Walk in all the ways I com-mand you, that it may go well with you.*        Jeremiah 7:23

### Thanks-giving For Our Covenant

Dad hesitated while he opened his Bible to find a verse. "Now you know why we have a Thanksgiving Day! In other countries where people don't know or love God there is no One to thank. Christians can thank their living God for all the love and planning He did. He gave a *new* covenant that will *never* grow old. Some day we'll talk about the beautiful promises and gifts He gives to His 'blood brothers' because of that Covenant…" Dad reached for our hands:

"I think God would like to watch us hold hands right now around the table… . Now I'll read what St. Paul wrote to some Christian friends on a day like this. He sent his letter to them with this prayer:

*But you have come to…Jesus the mediator of a new cov-enant, and to the sprinkled blood…May the God of peace, who through the blood of the eternal covenant brought back from the dead our Lord Jesus, that great Shepherd of the sheep, equip you with everything good for doing His will…*
Hebrews 12:22,24; 13:20-21

"Now let's all say together after me:

Dear Father in Heaven…
We thank You for everything.
We thank You for sending Jesus.
We thank You for Your Covenant.
We love You for Your love.

We thank You for each other.
Help us to be good children.
For Your glory, we praise You. Amen."

# Part II

# God's Give-Away Plans

# Chapter 7

# The Promises

*Through these He has given us His very great and precious promises, so that through them you may participate in the divine nature...*
2 Peter 1:4

*...Christ has become a servant of the Jews on behalf of God's truth, to confirm the promises made to the patriarchs so that the Gentiles may glorify God for His mercy...*
Romans 15:8-9

*For no matter how many promises God has made, they are "Yes" in Christ. And so through Him the "Amen" is spoken by us to the glory of God.*
2 Corinthians 1:20

*Since we have these promises, dear friends, let us purify ourselves from everything that contaminates body and spirit, perfecting holiness out of reverence for God.*
2 Corinthians 7:1

*Yet [Abraham] did not waver through unbelief regarding the promise of God, but was strengthened in his faith and gave glory to God, being fully persuaded that God had power to do what He had promised.*

Romans 4:20-21

*God is not a man, that He should lie, nor a son of man, that He should change His mind. Does He speak and then not act? Does He promise and not fulfill?*
Numbers 23:19

# God's Promises Are for Real

**A**ren't promises fun? Some are little ones and others are real big ones They keep us guessing because we wonder when they will really happen.

When I was a kid shooting marbles with my friend, I'd say, "Cross my heart, hope to die! If you give me five marbles I'll let you play with my guinea pig tomorrow! Honest Injun, I will!" then we'd slap each other's hands and we'd start our marble game (with me using five of his clay marbles). When I won four more, I'd offer to swap them for one glassy. "I'll give you four, I promise!" It made the game exciting. By making a promise that I would keep tomorrow, I had won a prized glassy today!

Of course, parents make bigger promises. Sometimes they remember them, and sometimes they don't. After all, they have a lot to think about. (At least that is what they say, don't they?) It keeps kids wondering which ones will be forgotten first, and which ones are bad promises!

### Forget the Bad Ones

In the supermarket I heard a teenage mother scream at her tired, little child: "You make one more noise and I'll kill you!" I saw a little lad standing by the liquor counter holding his knees tightly together in a half crouch: "Mommy, I gotta go...!" he said in a whimper.

"You shut up right now," she growled back, "or I'll kick you till you can't pee. Don't you see I'm buying Daddy his liquor?"

Such promises should never be kept! *Kids* know that. "If you eat one more cookie, you'll have appendicitis!" "You get your hands dirty one more time and I'll run 'em through the wringer: you'll learn." "You broke your father's coffee cup; he'll knock your teeth out tonight!"

Of course, God's plans have no such promises of terror. As our Bible tells us, all His promises are carried out to *His* glory; that means to His pleasure and *our* good. Besides, when He makes a promise, it will be carried out just like He says! All His promises to His children are made to be like lovely gifts. There are so many kinds of lambs that He has prepared special promises to meet each of their needs.

### Promises are "Give-Aways"

We could call the Bible the Book of Promises! It contains over 8,800 of them. Most are found in the Old Testament (Covenant) because that is the story of the times when people first needed help. When Jesus came to earth, He quickly fulfilled the *old* promises, so that there would be only a few *new* ones left for us to learn.

The reason that God makes them part of His Give-Away Plan is simple; He wants His children to have all of them *for free*. God didn't ever need the promises for Himself. He made them for *us* to use and enjoy right here on earth every day. We do not need to work *for* them; we only need to work *with* them! Jesus did the work and said: "It is finished." Isn't He a wonderful

Giver? He shares all His "goodies" besides promising more for tomorrow.

## A Pure Mind Makes Pure Promises

The Bible tells us that God is very special and unusual. One reason is that *His* thoughts are different from ours. Yes, our Heavenly Father thinks and works with a *pure* mind. That means that He makes no mistakes and that He cannot lie. Whatever He promises to do, He will carry out.

We are also told that His thoughts are *higher* than the heavens. When He thinks about someone like you, He has the facts firsthand. He knows all the little details. Then when He makes a promise, He never has to go back and change it. Sitting in Heaven, He has a real "bird's eye" view of every person He ever made; and that makes His promises pure and sure. (Children would say "right on!")

## Here Comes the Judge

One morning we had a special surprise at our house, my brother and I. Our Grandpa from way out west (he called it "Laramie") came to visit us. We had never seen him before that morning. His face sort of looked like some of the paintings of Moses in our book of biblical pictures. He was big. His voice sounded like a judge—so deep and sure and final. He stood straight and tall. Bob asked him: "What do you do, Grandpa?" "Why, I'm a judge, sonny," he said, as Mom added three more pancakes to his plate.

"You see, an honest judge never goes back on his word. Before he makes a promise, he first makes sure he can keep it; then he goes to work to make it happen! Your Daddy was once my little boy much like you. That doesn't seem possible, does it? (His chuckle sounded like an echo in an empty apple barrel from deep down.) Well, I promised him that I would come two thousand miles so these old eyes could see *his* fine boys!…Come here, let me hug you." He laid down his knife and fork, and held one of us on each knee. I thought he was looking right through me like he didn't want to forget a thing, ever.

By the end of the week I was *sure* that Gramp knew everything! He answered every question I could think of. We were surprised that he could be smart and old at the same time! We had been told by other kids who had grandpas that old folks were nutty, with loose teeth, and "no marbles in their heads." (They didn't know *this* grandpa, for sure!)

I could tell he loved our New England maple syrup on Mom's buckwheats. "Yessiree," he remarked, smacking his lips. "God was surely good to give my boy two find lads and a beautiful wife. I couldn't have planned it better myself! At my age He could not have sent me more excellent presents!"

### The Judge Picks an Apple

Grandpa was like a magnet. We kids wanted to be around him 'cause he kept saying things we didn't know. Luckily he sat down quite often, under the apple tree or on the stonewall or by the grape arbor. We guessed that he had a bad leg on the side he carried his cane, but he never said anything about it. Mostly he stopped walking wherever he saw a special flower or an apple graft or an oriole's nest like a little grass basket hung on a twig.

We would flop down at his feet to listen as he inspected a speckled apple. "Say, this is a beauty. Just look at those little white dots spaced evenly over the red skin! Don't you wonder how they knew where to go so we'd recognize it as a Baldwin pie apple? And look at that little knuckle on the stem, just where it would break off easily so as not to hurt the twig! How many apples do you suppose are in the seeds inside?" I quietly shrugged my shoulders so he wouldn't stop talking.

"Only one Person knows, sonny," he continued as he turned the apple over and over. "When God made apples, He spoke to the *seeds*! Oh yes, He can speak to anything He wants—apples, birds, donkeys, waves, clouds, the sun and moon! *Everything He* said was either a promise or a command—and it always came true! You see, He was a Lawyer and a Judge. When *He* spoke, *everything* listened!" He wiped the apple on his sleeve, and bit out a big chunk. "Yessiree! God made everything good, too."

I was bursting with questions inside. Since Gramp was busy chewing, I broke the silence: "But I don't understand; what could God promise an *apple*?" He looked down at me and swallowed.

"Richard, you remind me so much of your dad when he was your age! It's a good thing that I had him to practice on! He made me look up a lot of answers.... Out West we say, 'Tell it straight, pardner, or you lose!' " He chuckled with that deep barrel-sound again. "The answer is really simple because it is in the Book that God wrote for us to study. When He made living things, He did not ever want to do it all over again, so He commanded them the very first day to be fruitful and multiply abundantly! Then He added a most important command, one that contained His very *first* promise! I think I can quote it from memory:

> *And God said, Let the earth bring forth grass, the herb yielding seed, and the fruit tree yielding fruit after his kind, whose seed is in itself, upon the earth: and it was so. And the earth brought forth grass, and herb yielding seed after his kind, and the tree yielding fruit, whose seed was in itself, after his kind: and God saw that it was good.*   Genesis 1:11-12 KJV

"Two days later, God gave the very same instructions to His new animals and birds and fishes:

> *And God said, Let the earth bring forth the living creature after his kind, cattle, and creeping thing, and beast of the earth after his kind...and God saw that it was good."*
>                                            Genesis 1:24-25 KJV

### God Himself—Our Role Model

"You see, sonny, God promised the apple and *all* His living things, right from the beginning, that an apple would make apples, a bird would make a bird, and a fish would make a fish. Then He said the same thing the next day about a man. If somebody tells you in school that a monkey made a man, remember that's a joke; it's just *monkey business*. You see, God was not monkeying around when He finally decided to make His very best creation, ever! Oh no! He did not want His people to live and act like monkeys! Or any animal. He wanted man to be very, very good; very special; very wise, and very loving.

"Then He said to Himself [the Planner], and to His Son [the Lamb], and to His Spirit [the Worker], Let Us use *Ourselves* as the model. Yes, we will make man in Our own image! We will make him just a little lower than we are. We will give him authority over everything We have already created. In fact, I like that idea so much that I will promise him everything I own, if in return he will simply *love* Us! I won't even let him fail if he will believe Us, and do what We tell him. In addition, when he makes a mistake, I will forgive him and forget about it, if he asks *Us* to help him with his problem!

"Boys, if I were sitting in the courthouse right now, I would slam my gavel and declare 'Court recessed! The evidence is overwhelming. I rule in favor of GOD!' "

### America—God's Gift

Of course, I could not have Grandpa all to myself. He wanted to take us kids to "places of historical interest" in Massachusetts. "Freedom was won with the blood of our ancestors on these very east coast battlefields," he told us. "If it hadn't been for praying mothers and real 'he-man fathers' who wanted their boys and girls 'to be free from tyranny,' we wouldn't have 'America, the Beautiful' as our own home of the brave!" (Grandpa lived "on the frontier" and he was very definite about some things, we discovered.) "If our people ever get softheaded and yellow-spined, or if they take off like mavericks instead of sticking together, this country will fold! God gave it to us as a gift to use, not abuse," he explained. "God said that He treats all nations alike; if we do not learn the lessons of history, then we will suffer their same mistakes!"

He held our hands as we walked around Bunker Hill Monument. "America didn't just happen, boys! It was earned. Brave men fought for it. Right here and in many other places. They were willing to *die* so their children could be free from injustices and tyranny. They wanted a nation where God would be worshiped even outdoors! Fathers wanted freedom to teach their children about God who *loves* people no matter which church building they enter. They wanted a place where their families could live in peace and their wives would be safe. They said 'We'll fight for God and country!' and they won with His help!"

### Land Of Promise or Land Of Problems

We could feel his pride oozing out through his big hardened hands. Somehow we knew that he and God were getting the job done of "winning the West." He told us that the frontier was still young and needed "lots of tending," but that it held tremendous promise for "us young-uns" once we were old enough and strong enough to take over. "Remember, boys, this is *God's* country. We didn't make it. He simple lets us *use* it. He will bless it as long as our people keep faith with Him. He told King David once to write down some promises. Here is one:

> *Blessed is the nation whose God is the Lord, the people He chose for His inheritance.*                    Psalm 33:12

"God also told King Solomon:

> *Righteousness exalts a nation, but sin is a disgrace to any people.*                    Proverbs 14:34

"Boys, the lessons of history prove that God *always* means what He says. I pray for your sakes and mine that our great nation never becomes a disgrace to God! Jesus will have to make a terrible judgment someday. We call it a 'ruling' in court. He predicted that some-time all the nations would be assembled before Him. He would divide them into two groups: sheep and goats. The sheep love Him but the goats hate Him. You can find the story in Matthew 25. It says that Jesus will bang down His gavel and point to the goats! 'You cursed people,' He will say, 'You disobeyed Me! Depart from Me...into everlasting fire, prepared for the devil and his angels.'

"We *must* pray, and so *must* our friends and every father and mother and government official, that our Land of the Free will not become a nation of *goats*! *We don't have to*. God promises to bless us if we simply be-have...Let's flag down the next carriage and take a ride to the Old North Church. I want to see that famous belfry before the sun goes down."

### A Life Lost for Lambs

Several years later we kids (then boys out of college) received telegrams that Judge Eby had suddenly dropped dead while trying to save dozens of little freezing lambs on his sheep farm in Minnesota. Hearing of the sudden storm and freezing winds, he had driven from Wyoming despite doctors' orders. With cane in hand, he had stumped across the stony fields in search of his little friends. Like his own Shepherd, he literally gave his life for lost lambs. How like Grandpa, we thought, to love lambs more than self.

Not for years would we kids realize the legacy (that means *give-aways*) that this Gramp had left behind. He loved to tell us about God's promises whenever we found time to "counsel" by a berry patch or under a shade tree. "You simply can't live sensibly," he had kept telling us, "unless you know what your promises are! And they are all FREE! God has never sent one person a bill for making him a promise. Nor can you work for one! All promises are gifts from the Father above to His children down here. The Bible says God works in the nighttime so you can have joy in the morning! Yessiree. He loves us so much that He wants us to have a Christmas every day! King David called God's promises *benefits*, and he said, 'Don't you forget them!' "

As we grew older it became obvious that the *prepared* Promises which God had put in His Lay-Away Plan become the *completed* Promises that we get from His Give-Away Plan. Our Father had it all figured out before we got here. That way He could start handing out His promised gifts as soon as we would ask! Jesus said that we should *ask, seek,* or *knock*. He said if we didn't, *nothing* would happen. He said that His Father always was waiting and waiting and *waiting* to hear from us!

### Promises Too Many to Count

It was not long before we boys discovered that our Heavenly Father had given us *more* promises than we could even write down on our ruled school paper. So we took Dad's suggestion to pick out a few promises from God's Word. "Make them your memory verses." That worked fine. Whenever we needed a new promise for some "big deal" at school or at camp or even at play, we could take the *right* one from our memory bank. Besides, it didn't cost a penny to learn a verse, or use it!

It was an exciting game to learn how many things God had promised us. For instance He offered us:

LOVE: God loved the world...
PEACE: I give you My peace...
COMFORT: I send you My Comforter...
GRACE: By grace you are saved through faith...
ABILITIES: All things are possible...
WISDOM: Whoever hears My sayings is wise...
SECURITY: You shall remain in My love...
FRIENDSHIP: You are My friends...
ETERNAL LIFE: Whoever believes has eternal
    life...
SALVATION: He who believes shall be saved...
INDWELLING: He dwells in Me and I in him...
RESURRECTION: I will raise him up on the last
    day...
HOLY SPIRIT: Your Heavenly Father shall give
    you...
COMPANIONSHIP: I am with you always...

We discovered hundreds of other promises in the Bible that God has given us. Here are a few for everyday use. (They work; we tried them out.):

HEALING: Lay on hands, and they will recover...
JOY: Ask, that your joy may be full...
SIGNS AND WONDERS: Will follow those who
    believe...
POWER: I give you power...
SAFETY: Nothing shall by any means hurt you...
FREEDOM: You shall be free indeed...

PROSPERITY: Give and it will be given unto
    you...
GREATER WORKS: Greater works shall he do...
STRENGTH: God is our refuge and strength...
QUIETNESS: He gives quietness...
PATIENCE: Testing of your faith works patience...
DELIVERANCE: He will make a way of escape...
VICTORY: Be of good cheer; I have overcome...

Some days we found "things were really tough." The teachers poured on the extra homework right when we had planned to go fishing. The grass seemed to need extra mowing just when the circus came to town. Or we had to cut firewood after school instead of skating.

It would have been awfully hard to grow up if we had not had promises to "try out." We kids wanted childish fun and play out of life. It took a while to discover that the greatest fun and joy came from using the promises every day, while we worked or played or studied.

You will have fun and joy, too, when you add the promises from God to all the other things you enjoy every day. Try being a *happy* lamb for one whole day, and you will want to be one *every* day. That's a *promise*!

# Chapter 8

# The New Life

*Therefore, if anyone is in Christ, he is a new creation; the old has gone, the new has come!*                    2 Corinthians 5:17

*...just as Christ was raised from the dead through the glory of the Father, we too may live a new life.*                    Romans 6:4

*...the gift of God is eternal life in Christ Jesus our Lord.*

Romans 6:23

*...God has given us eternal life, and this life is in His Son.*

1 John 5:11

*For God so loved the world that He gave His one and only Son, that whoever believes in Him shall not perish but have eternal life.*

John 3:16

*...whoever hears My word and believes Him who sent Me has eternal life and will not be condemned; he has crossed over from death to life.*                    John 5:24

*...no one can see the kingdom of God unless he is born again.*

John 3:3

*...you have taken off your old self with its practices and have put on the new self, which is being renewed in knowledge in the image of its Creator.*                    Colossians 3:9-10

# A Worm
# That Flies

**T**he meadow behind our home was a constant source of discovery and wonder. It was simply alive with exciting things. After the first rains that melted the last lumps of lingering snow, we found fuzzy little green "violin handles" pushing up through the matted grass. They turned into lovely ferns in a few days. Almost overnight little blue violets peeked out from beneath the heart-shaped leaves that shaded them. And frightened green 'hoppers shot through the air as we pulled up grassy clods in search of nightcrawlers. Adder's tongues and trilliums and mayflowers had races to be the first to bloom.

Bob and I had a favorite "weed." It started out as a little circle of furry leaves. Then a stalk shot up from the center and ended up taller than we were. It carried some velvety leaves up with it. By summertime it was prickly and sticky with fat teardrop pods around the top. When the first frost touched them, they exploded and released a cloud of feathery parachutes that blew across the fields like the first snowflakes of fall. We loved to chase them: The winner had to catch the most! But that was not the only reason we loved milkweeds.

One day while playing hide-and-seek in the milkweeds we discovered they grew worms? Furry ones. *Caterpillars*, someone called them. They rippled as they walked along the stems, with their red-brown hairs looking like tiny costumes. Then a week later in place of the pretty *'pillars* we found only shiny, smooth, grey-green, little hard things hanging by a thread under the milkweed leaves.

Mother was waiting when we arrived out of breath with a leaf in each hand. "Mommie, the caterpillars are all gone today; look what they left. What are they anyway?"

"I could tell you, boys, but let's put them in a Mason jar with mosquito netting over the top. Let's see who will be the first to discover the answer!" (Mother had taught other little boys and she knew that *patience* is an important part of learning.) "Don't water it; just let it alone."

A week later I heard Bob squeal with excitement. He charged around the corner of the porch carrying his canning jar. "Look, someone put a red butterfly in my bottle. It has a little trick-or-treat whistle in its mouth. Wowee, it's pretty!" Mother stood smiling at the door; "What happened to the little grey thing on the leaf, Robert?" she said.

"It's all cracked. It's empty! How come, Mom? I didn't break it, honest I didn't."

"Of course not," Mom reassured him. "You have just learned one of the most amazing lessons in all of nature. Your Monarch caterpillar somehow decided to shrivel up and become a dried-up, dead-looking chrysalis. Then after it slept for a while it decided to bring joy to the world and come back to life in a form that could fly and flutter and make children laugh.... That curled-up "trick-or-treat whistle" is its little drinking straw so it can smell and taste its favorite sweet juices in the throats of the flowers. It has changed from a kind of worm into a kind of angel. It doesn't have to eat any more, or crawl on its stomach. It is free to fly into the sky!"

We couldn't understand what we were seeing. Even the warm corn bread and clover honey for lunch could not distract our gaze from the four-inch butterfly that came out of a little one-inch shell. It didn't make sense— a worm that could fly. Where did its fur go, and those sharp teeth that ate leaves? "Hey, Mom, how'd he do it?"

### New Life from Old—Really?

Several years later we began to understand how caterpillars help to explain God's Give-Away Plan. One of His promises says that He wants His children to have "new life" when they grow up. In His Book He says that they should shed their *childish things* and *childish words* when they grow up. He says that this would happen to them when they became "new creatures." There had been one big problem: No one but God knew how to make a "new creature." So He decided to do the job Himself by making a *gift* of "new life" to all who would simply accept it. Then they would be "new creatures" with a "new spirit" in them! God said that we could have this gift for free—on one condition— that we would let His Son Jesus be our Lord and Master. If so, Jesus would be our Lamb too!

God knew that children would find this miracle (of becoming someone new) hard to understand. Let us suppose that one day God decided to explain it this way: "I will give My children a simple illustration of how I can change them into *new* creatures with a *new* way of life! I will make butterflies out of worms! Instead of having to spend their lives eating leaves all the time just to stay alive, I will let their old natures die. Then I will let them come alive with a *new* spirit!

"Instead of living like worms, they can then soar like eagles toward My heavens. Instead of crawling on their bellies and grinding their teeth all day and night, they can be beautiful and free, full of joy, and fed with nectar! For My children I will let My dear Lamb die in their place, and be wrapped like a chrysalis, and then come forth in a *new* body that can rise up into My Heaven! That way, *My* children who believe in Jesus and Me won't have to get into grave clothes, but can become 'new creatures' in Christ Jesus without their spirits dying!"

God went right ahead with His idea; and Jesus was obedient and died and arose for us a long time ago. Then He told us in His Book to "put on [become] the NEW MAN" whom He created (remade) into righteousness and holiness like God (Eph. 4:24)! God even says that we have a NEW MIND when we are NEW CREATURES in Jesus (Eph. 4:23). We have a NEW SPIRIT too. In fact, we have a NEW LIFE in us that makes us want to do what pleases God, now that He is our Father!

His children are so fortunate. With this gift of NEW LIFE they can ask their Father in Heaven to let His Kingdom come now so His will can be done in us right on earth as though we were already in Heaven! Let's ask Him to do it!

## New Life Is a Gift If You Take It

To some children, God's Plan may seem hard to understand. But it really isn't. The whole secret is to know from the start that God would not be God at all unless He could make butterflies out of worms. If He couldn't do that, then He certainly could not even make a baby, or a star, or a raindrop, or a sunbeam. Worse yet, He couldn't make smiles or happiness or tender hands to hold cuddly things or Christmas dollies. But He does all these things!

Since He can do everything that needs to be done, He can even love people and children who don't deserve it. He can make crybabies smile. He can make crabby little girls into happy helpers around the house. He can make grumpy boys into grateful, beaming buddies. Best of all, He can teach His children how to *love* one another.

LIFE is His favorite Give-Away Gift. He calls it His ETERNAL LIFE because it lets His children live with Him forever. His children call it NEW LIFE, because it makes them new inside and they feel good all over. When they *ask* Jesus into their hearts, He sends the Holy Spirit into them to give them the power of the NEW LIFE. They feel like they could fly all of a sudden, because they are new and clean and full of joy.

Wouldn't you like to feel that way? If you want the most that God can give you *today*, just ask. You can say something this simple:

Dear God in Heaven, I want to be a child of Yours.
I want to love people. Forgive me for being unkind and angry so often. I want to be like new all

over. I believe that Jesus came to save and help me. I want Him to be my Friend and my Shepherd, starting today. Thank You, Father for being so good. Amen. Oh yes, I'll talk to You again later. Right now I'll start enjoying my new life!

If you said this little prayer and meant it, you have a new partner all at once. He is God Himself. Now you are ready for some more of His Give-Aways...they are all a part of the tale of love between the two of you.

# Chapter 9

# The New Mind

*Your attitude should be the same as that of Christ Jesus...*[who] *being found in appearance as a man, He humbled Himself and became obedient to death—even death on a cross!*    Philippians 2:5,8

*Then make my joy complete by being like-minded, having the same love, being one in spirit and purpose.*    Philippians 2:2

*"For who has known the mind of the Lord that he may instruct Him?" But we have the mind of Christ.*    1 Corinthians 2:16

*We have not received the spirit of the world but the Spirit who is from God, that we may understand what God has freely given us.*

1 Corinthians 2:12

*...everything that I learned from My Father I have made known to you.*    John 15:15

*Evil men do not understand justice, but those who seek the Lord understand it fully.*    Proverbs 28:5

*[Jesus] replied, "The knowledge of the secrets of the kingdom of heaven has been given to you, but not to them* [unbelievers]. *"*

Matthew 13:11

# Your New Memory Bank

**T**he way people were acting around Jesus, and the way that ancient peoples had behaved, gave God proof enough that humans needed a *new mind*! King Solomon was shocked when he saw unholy men pretending to offer sacrifices to make themselves look honest. He wrote:

*The sacrifice of the wicked is an abomination (that means a terrible deed): how much more, when he bringeth it with a wicked mind!* Proverbs 21:27 KJV

You may remember that Jesus saw this very thing happening in the Temple the day He overturned the tables of the deceitful moneychangers who changed sacrifices into commerce! (That means they tried to sell godliness for money.)

Another day King Solomon listened to the gangs shouting at each other in the streets. He went home and wrote: "The fool uttereth *all* his mind." Centuries later, Jesus told the mobs: "You know not what you say!" And St. Paul reminded his friends that "the carnal (old) mind is enmity (an affront) against God." Today we could say that our unclean minds are like some computers: "Garbage in, garbage out!" If our minds look that way to us, just imagine how they appear to God!

Yes, we do need *new minds* is we are to be *God's* children!

The *new mind* is really not hard for a child to understand once he is told what he thinks with. Let me tell you quite simply: your mind is something like your radio or television. What you see and hear coming from the "stations" on the dial was fed into the cameras and microphones. Some of the sounds and pictures went straight through the air to your house where you heard the program right away. Most of the time, however, the little electrical waves were captured on tapes and stored in the station for later use. You have heard of "memory banks." They are a kind of man-made *mind*.

Well, your mind is a memory bank for all sorts of information and feelings. Your eyes feed pictures into your mind, your ears feed sounds, and your skin feeds feelings like "ouch" or warmth! Your tongue feeds sweetness and sour tastes. All of your beautiful body is feeding sensations into your mind every minute. You wouldn't believe how busy your "insides" are all day long, telling your mind how to digest french fries, or play hopscotch, or catch a baseball. Sometimes your body says, "A bee just stung me," and your mind tells your mouth to shout "Ouch!" Then it tells your eyes to cry, and tells your feet to run and let Mother hug you! You have a wonderful mind—as long as you keep it shined up and clean and healthy and happy.

### God's Garage Has New Parts

A baby is something like a new car. The face is shiny, and the motor runs smoothly. The pink skin has a fresh "paint job," and the morning "wash" brings giggly smiles. The little hands and feet reach out and kick in eagerness to get going. The mind begins listening for the "daily news" about mealtimes, family reactions, kittie's purring, and new diapers. Like a sponge, the active brain is soaking up every bit of information that passes by. In a few months the mind begins to store other strange things it hears and sees and feels.

The cleanness and the newness of the little mind begins to be tarnished by all kinds of dirt and fears and disappointments. Children start to *cry* for things instead of *ask* for them. They have heard "No" so often that they start saying it back to Mom and Dad. Then they get spanked, and that makes them angry at first, and they start screaming or throwing tantrums. Or they sulk and pout to get attention. In time their minds get badly tangled up like a kitten rolling in a ball of yarn. Untruths creep in like spiders which spin cobwebs over the brain just so children cannot be sure what is right and what is wrong. Before long, every child needs a *new mind*.

### Jesus and Satan Both Want Your Mind

All the time this trouble is brewing, God is asking His children to let *Him* unravel their minds. God's enemy, satan, is roaring at them not to listen for one minute. This is called "the battle for men's minds"; it never ceases—all their lives. *God* offers "love, power, and a *sound mind*" to every one of His children, little or big, young or old. But *satan* offers only lies, deceit, sorrow, and tears. *God* says, "Follow Me, and I will give you love and peace and rest (mental joys)." *Satan* says, "Follow me, and I will give you thrills and will let you do your own thing!"

God says, "Everything I own will be yours for free; Jesus paid the bill already *for you.*" *Satan* says, "Work for me all your life, and when you die that's it." (He doesn't even dare tell them about his home in Hell where he can never put out the fire.) Satan says, "You are already smarter than God because you know evil and filth, and have a clever mind which can get you more than God has for you!" *God* says, "I will wash you (your mind) white as snow if you will ask Me to! In fact, My child, I will do even better because I love you so; I will make you a *new creature* with a *new mind* so you can start life all over! *Let Me be your Teacher* so I can erase the mistakes on your blackboard. My answers will give you all A's!"

## The First Thing To Do

This is when the fun begins: You can take your mind (at any age) to God's Garage. He already knows what is wrong with you because He made you on His assembly line, and He has the blueprints! (Ask your folks to read you about God's Plan for your body and mind in Psalms 139:15-18.)

The first thing He does is wash you. Your mind has been full of sticky old mud (called sin), and it comes loose when God's fresh water hits it. The Lord says: "Though your sins are like scarlet, they shall be as white as snow" (Is. 1:18b). King David asked God to "Wash me, and I will be whiter than snow" (Ps. 51:7b). You wouldn't think that a great king needed washing, would you? His mind had gotten dirty, and he knew it!

One of Jesus' closest friends tells us in his book how Jesus washes away sin. Fisherman John wrote: "The blood of Jesus, His Son, purifies us from every sin" (1 John 1:7). That means that *He* must do it all, because *we* do not have anything for washing our own minds clean, do we?

### The Second Thing...

It would not do much good for you to have a clean mind if it were empty, would it? God knows that too. The second thing He must do (once you let Him) is to put you up on the hydraulic jack like the garageman does your car. God loves to lift you above the troubles you have had. Both of you can see better that way: He can see your needs, and you can see His hands at work! After all, He has been a body mechanic long before autos were invented, and He knows right where to start fixing your groans and squeaks. His second job is to give you one more of His Give-Aways, a *new mind*. The parts of your old mind that were good enough to keep (the clean and working parts), He simply *renews* with His cleanser and polisher (Jesus' blood). Then He adds *some* of His power (you could not handle *all* of His power right away). He gets ready to charge your battery!

The Bible tells us that He works this miracle like a transformer! You have several at home: they all do the same thing. In one end goes a powerful voltage of electricity, and out of the other end comes just the right amount to run your radio, or Dad's shaver, or Mom's hair dryer or a recorder. God is like that. He has *all* the power in the world *in* Him, but He lets *us* have just the *right amount* to run our minds and our bodies. He calls it *renewing* (like recharging) our minds: "Be transformed by the *renewing* of your mind." Why? "...That ye may prove [experience] what is that good, and acceptable, and perfect, will of God" (Rom. 12:2 KJV).

### The Third Thing...

Now that Jesus has cleaned up the old mind and has transformed it with His power, He then reaches into His Give-Away toolkit again and pulls out the *best gift* of all; God's MIND, the SPIRIT! Can you imagine Him giving us His own Mind to use whenever we are willing to? This is called the *new mind*; it is the *mind of Christ*. And He shares it with His little lambs!

When God looks into our hearts and minds after this miracle, He sees the *mind* of the Spirit at work, praying that God's wonderful will *can* happen every day right inside us! The Bible says:

> ...*the Spirit helps us in our weakness. We do not know what we ought to pray, but the Spirit Himself intercedes for us with groans that words cannot express. And He who searches our hearts knows the mind of the Spirit, because the Spirit intercedes for the saints in accordance with God's will.*
>
> Romans 8:26-27

Children have to learn how to use this *new mind* every day, instead of that old dirty one. It is really fun, but it takes patience. Jesus helps you to think straight and speak kindly. He even stops nightmares and gives you sweet dreams instead. He makes you want to smile, and sing, and dance for joy. He makes you and Him just *one*.

Even when St. Paul was chained in a damp dungeon all day by himself, he was so happy with his *new mind* that he wrote his friends in faraway Philippi and told them that if they had this *peaceful* kind of mind then they could complete his joy "by being like-minded, having the same love [Jesus'], being one in spirit [desire] and purpose [mind]" (Phil. 2:1-2). He told his friends over in Corinth that if they loved Jesus, they already had the *mind* of Christ!

## The Main Thing

Wouldn't it be foolish to have a new gift and not use it? Children would be laughed at if they hid their Christmas crayons, or didn't try out the new bicycle or their new roller skates! What good would a watch be if it were never wound? Or dancing slippers if never worn? It would be foolish not be enjoy the *New Mind* that God gives us so we can enjoy Him. The main thing about God's gifts is that they need to be used and shared. Besides, they never can be used up; they are forever!

## The Joyful Thing

As you practice using *your* renewed mind, you discover that there is so much to know and enjoy about your *new mind*. You *know* that it is *God's* gift to you because you are in love with His Son Jesus. You *know* that this Spirit of God tells your *new mind* how to work and what to think and how to speak. You can already have whatever you need from God if you let your *new mind* talk with Him and listen to His answers. That is what it is for: *knowing* for sure that His Give-Away Plan includes all your needs: wisdom, joy, comfort, peace, hope, and lots of love!

Finally, children, the gift of *your new mind* is meant to be used every day for one main purpose: "That ye may with *one mind* and one mouth glorify God, even the Father of our Lord Jesus Christ!" (Rom. 15:6 KJV).

Then we are told to: "...receive *ye one another*, as Christ also received us to the glory of God" (Rom. 15:7 KJV).

That means that we must behave like Jesus did when He went about town loving people like they were lambs! He said, "A new commandment I give unto you, That ye love one another, as I have loved you..." (Jn. 13:34). With your *new mind*, loving people is easy. It makes others happy, and you too!

## The Last Thing

The last thing to remember about your *new mind* is this: It was *given* to *you* by God. Do not throw it away. The Holy Spirit of God wants you to use it to change your life from failure to success. (That is just what you are wanting every day, isn't it?) *You* want love and joy.

Even though God's Bible uses some big words to tell us about His reasons for giving us so many gifts, most children can understand *this*: His instructions about using their *new mind*. "Set your minds on things above, not on earthly things" (Col. 3:2). That means for us to love God's way of thinking instead of our naughty ways. God explains it this way: "For to be carnally minded [dirty-minded and full of hate] is death [in the long run], but to be spiritually minded [using the *new mind*] is life and peace" (Rom. 8:6 KJV). That is just what you want, isn't it? God gives you His permission to use His mind all *for free*!

Your *old* mind (before you loved Jesus) thought that God's promises were "foolishness." But your *new mind* tells you that Jesus lives *inside* you now. You can play and work and study, and He will make everything turn out OK!

## Sign-out Instructions

When you leave the garage, Jesus hands you your instructions. He has fixed your mixed-up mind; He has charged your battery with His power; He has filled your tank with His Spirit; and now He says, "Take good care of your *body!*"

Jesus made your body to work, for Him and for all persons around you (He calls them your "neighbors"). He is upset when you let your body do foolish things, like swearing, or hurting people, or swallowing poisonous drugs, or going to bad places where you would be ashamed to be found. Now that you are a King's Kid with a *new mind*, He has a special set of rules for you to follow. They are really simple, because He helps you do them automatically if you let Him.

One rule says: "Come to Me," whenever you are in trouble, "and I will help you." That means that He is ready to help your mind work better, make your body well, and supply your needs. Of course you have to come and ask Him *first!*

Another rule says: "Love God." That is easy when you realize all He is doing for you each day. Another rule says: "Love your neighbor as yourself." This is not so easy because you have to pretend that *you are* your neighbor so you can understand his or her mind. But you *can* learn how to love! You have the *new mind*! It's fun.

Jesus has summed up all His instructions for using this wonderful mind and body and soul that He made for us! Here is what we are told:

*Therefore, I urge you, brothers, in view of God's mercy, to offer your bodies as living sacrifices, holy and pleasing to God—this is your spiritual act of worship. Do not conform any longer to the pattern of this world, but be transformed by the renewing of your mind. Then you will be able to test and approve what God's will is—His good, pleasing and perfect will.*                                                    **Romans 12:1-2**

# Chapter 10

# The New Fruit

*For the fruit of the light consists in all goodness, righteousness and truth.*                                                            Ephesians 5:9

*When the harvest time approached, he sent his servants to the tenants to collect his fruit.*                                          Matthew 21:34

*Remember this: Whoever sows sparingly will also reap sparingly, and whoever sows generously will also reap generously.*

2 Corinthians 9:6

*The hardworking farmer should be the first to receive a share of the crops.*                                                              2 Timothy 2:6

*Do not be deceived: God cannot be mocked. A man reaps what he sows.*                                                                    Galatians 6:7

*...every tree that does not produce good fruit will be cut down and thrown into the fire.*                                                   Luke 3:9

*...the wisdom that comes from heaven is first of all pure; then peace-loving, considerate, submissive, full of mercy and good fruit, impartial and sincere.*                                                  James 3:17

*...the fruit of the Spirit is love, joy, peace, patience, kindness, goodness, faithfulness, gentleness and self-control.*     Galatians 5:22-23a

# Fruit Comes in Two Kinds

**E**ven as children we have learned that fruits are of two kinds: Some are sweet, others sour. Some are fresh, others are rotten inside. Some have ripened, but others are still green. God knows that there are also two other kinds of fruit: He calls some of them *good*, but others are *evil*. We discovered that these fruits result from our behavior. God has explained that people can tell whether we are King's Kids (God's children) by simply watching our behavior toward others. The Bible calls our behavior our "fruits."

*...by their fruits ye shall know them.*     Matthew 7:20 KJV

Jesus said that we grow much like trees. We need light and water and food and good soil, He said. The reason He knew so much about gardening and people was that He Himself was the first Gardener! He had His own garden called Eden which He loaned to Adam and Eve. They refused to take gardening lessons, and it became overgrown with weeds and pests! (*Spiritual* weeds and pests are called *sin*.)

For the same reason, He knows all about the fruits of *people*—our deeds. (Jesus made our mothers and fathers, too. Like Him, they can easily tell when children are not behaving!) Jesus said that *wise* children honor (listen to) their parents so as to learn quickly how to live happy and longer lives. A wonderful thing happens when children obey their parents: the whole family *falls in love* with each other. God meant families to be that way!

### The Evil Fruit of Satan

A real problem with fruit started way back when there were only two people on earth: Adam and Eve were the names that God gave them. He had created them with clean minds and hearts so they could behave like God's children should. There was only one thing that God told them not to do: "Don't experiment with evil!" (He explained that satan had once tried being evil in Heaven, and had been "kicked out.") He said, "I am a righteous God, so I must treat everyone the same. That tree over there has the fruit of wickedness on it. Do not eat any!"

Well, can you believe this? Their Creator had hardly disappeared through the garden gate before satan came and whispered in Eve's ear: "Hello, Beautiful. You can be smarter than Adam if you eat that fruit! Afterwards Adam can eat some, and both of you will be as smart as I am. Don't be a dummy. It tastes good. I wouldn't fool you, now, would I?"

Eve probably hesitated for a moment because God had said they would *surely die* if they ate wicked fruit. But satan was smiling so sweetly that he looked like an angel of light! Eve figured that there was one sure way to find out who was right, God or satan. So she took a bite! And gave a slice to Adam.

We know the rest of the story. *God* was right! Their minds learned about evil. They did die, and all their descendants after them, because evil destroyed them. Satan's fruit is rotten—it poisons people's lives and makes them disobey God. King David said that God's enemies would be destroyed by fire, and "their fruit [idol worship] shalt Thou destroy from the earth" (Ps. 21:10 KJV). His son, King Solomon, said that people who refuse God's advice shall "...eat of the fruit of their *own* way" and *perish* (Prov. 1:31 KJV). He told his friends also that "the *fruit of the wicked* [leads] to *sin*" (Prov. 10:16 KJV). It is clear that our God does not approve of His children bearing or even touching "rotten fruit."

In fact, the ancient prophet Jeremiah heard God say to all the nations of the earth:

*...I am bringing disaster on this people, the fruit of their schemes, because they have not listened to My words and have rejected My law.*                              Jeremiah 6:19

Then he heard God give a warning:

*The heart is deceitful above all things and beyond cure. Who can understand it? I the Lord search the heart and examine the mind, to reward a man according to his conduct, according to what his deeds* [the fruit of his doings] *deserve.*
                                        Jeremiah 17:9-10

Finally, God told the people who called Him a liar:

*I am against you...I will punish you as your deeds deserve, declares the Lord.*                              Jeremiah 21:13-14

He said He would build a fire of wood that would devour everything around it. (Goodbye, rotten fruit!) God gives His children only new, fresh fruit!

A new creature bears the fruit of the Spirit who is *inside* him. It is fresh fruit for us and our neighbors to enjoy. It comes in *flavors*.

### Fruit Flavor #1: LOVE

Because our God is Love, He gives us this flavor first. It is His best fruit because it flavors all the others.

He says that without love we "become as sounding brass, or a tinkling cymbal." Without love He tells us that we are nothing. Even when we work our fingers to the bone being busybodies, He says that it amounts to nothing unless done in love. He says that love is even greater than faith and hope.

Of course, *children* know this is true, don't they? Little boys know that those drooly kisses from neighbor ladies do not always mean "I love you"; sometimes they mean, "I hope you don't chase baseballs through my flower garden." It might mean: "If you haven't moved away by Christmas, I'll *have* to buy you another gift." Even when brother or sister hugs you at the birthday party, you figure they are thinking, "Your party is better than mine was. How come?"

Our Father is like this: He wants our days to be filled with love—the kind that *heals hurts!* He shows us how to love others: He loved people *before* they even loved Him. The Bible says He loved us *first* (1 John 4:19). That is why He gave us Jesus to save us from satan who does not love us at all! St. John explains that "love comes from God," and "everyone who loves has been born of God" (that makes him a *new* creature or a reborn child). We are told that "since God so loved us, we also ought to love one another" (1 John 4:11). "If we love one another, God lives in us…and…we live in Him…" (1 John 4:12b-13).

That is the kind of conduct that makes our Heavenly Father proud of us each day. People's eyes cannot *see* God loving them, but they can watch us instead—being kind at school, loving our parents, helping old people get around, sharing our time with someone who needs a little love. God's Bible says: "And He has given us this command: Whoever loves God must also love his brother [another person]" (1 John 4:21).

It may seem funny that God calls us "trees" (Ps. 1), and Jesus calls us "branches" of the Vine. The reason is that both trees and vines are expected to bear fruit. When they don't, they are pulled up and burned. Like trees and vines, we must grow little lovebuds all over us every day! Jesus says *there is no better fruit* than love.

### Fruit Flavor #2: JOY

The second jar of fruit on God's shelf is labeled Joy. It is so tasty that people hunt all over the world for it. Strangely enough, many of the joys in the world turn out to be only imitations of the real thing. Some kinds of fruit bring a temporary joy (for a moment or two), but then the flavor turns sour.

We have to be so careful to look at the "tree" before we sample its fruit; it may have a harmful spirit in it. It might be poison even though it has a joyful taste at first.

I remember that St. John warned God's children to be on the lookout for counterfeits:

*Dear friends, do not believe every spirit, but test the spirits to see whether they are from God, because many false prophets* [bad trees] *have gone out into the world...Every spirit that does not acknowledge Jesus is not from God...This is how we recognize the Spirit of truth and the spirit of falsehood.*
1 John 4:1,3,6

The *real* joy is the fruit from Jesus' lips. He told His disciples first about love, then about joy. He explained why:

*I have told you this so that My joy may be in you and that*
*your joy may be complete.*                          John 15:11

Jesus told them that even after He went back to
Heaven He would return: "But I will see you again and
you will rejoice, and no one will take away your joy"
(Jn. 16:22b).

Even the angel at Bethlehem knew how much joy
had suddenly come to earth on the first Christmas eve:

*Do not be afraid, I bring you good news of **great joy** that will*
*be for all the people. Today in the town of David a Savior has*
*been born to you; He is CHRIST THE LORD.*
                                              Luke 2:10b-11

God's Word says so very much about joy that we
can imagine His "joy orchard" as being always *loaded*
with fruit! His children are invited to eat them *all*:

"Joy of the Lord"—your strength, Nehemiah 8:10
"Shouts of joy"—your defense, Psalm 5:11 KJV
"Fullness of joy"—in His presence, Psalm 16:11 KJV
"Sacrifices of joy"—in His temple, Psalm 27:6
"Joy in the morning"—after weeping, Psalm 30:5
"God, my exceeding joy"—at the altar, Psalm 43:4
"Joy of the whole earth"—city of God, Psalm 48:2
"Joy of a wise child"—parenthood, Proverbs
    23:24
"Sing for joy of heart"—God's servants, Isaiah
    65:14
"Enter…into the joy of the Lord"—Heaven, Mat-
    thew 25:21
"Joy in the Holy Spirit"—Kingdom of God,
    Romans 14:17
"Joy unspeakable"—belief in Jesus, 1 Peter 1:8

Don't you feel sorry for the millions of people without joy? If they simply knew enough about Jesus to love Him, they could enjoy these fantastic promises about joy. The Bible says:

> ...[Jesus] *is able to keep you from falling* [making mistakes], *and to present you faultless before the presence of His glory with exceeding joy.*  Jude 24 KJV

> *And these things write we unto you, that your joy may be full.*  1 John 1:4 KJV

We are never too young or too small for God to use us. If we can speak, even in sign language, someone can understand us when we say "Jesus loves *you*, too!" God will let someone hear you, and will give that new friend a "dose" of faith so he will let Jesus into his heart too! Then the fruit of joy will be in your hands when Jesus comes:

> *For what is our hope, our joy, or the crown in which we will glory in the presence of our Lord Jesus when He comes? Is it not you* [converts]*? Indeed, you are our glory and joy.*  1 Thessalonians 2:19-20

Bringing someone to Jesus should be all the fruit we need! But the Spirit has more.

### Fruit flavor #3: PEACE

The flavor of God's Peace cannot be described! The Bible says it "passes understanding." The Spirit wanted it that way so that God's children could have a praising contest. Each little lamb in His green pastures would graze beside the peaceful waters, see himself in the still pools, and say to his Shepherd, "Baaaa!" In lamb's language that means "Father, I thank You for this *peace.*"

All God's creatures seek peace. But there is never any peace on earth unless Jesus is present. When He was born, a multitude of angels announced that peace was *on earth at last.*

Isaiah had foretold the coming of this Prince of Peace 700 years before. He said that Jesus would "publish peace" (declare the Good News). But people were too selfish and greedy to accept God's gift of peace: they shouted "Peace! Peace!" in their political meetings, but there was *no peace in their hearts.* (They still do it!)

When Jesus' time on earth was ending, He told His disciples that He was going back to Heaven, and He was giving them something special to remember Him by:

> *Peace I leave with you; My peace I give you. I do not give to you as the world gives. Do not let your hearts be troubled...*
> John 14:27

Peace is probably the *smoothest* flavor of all the fruits of the Spirit. It just seems to flow like honey all through us. It does for us what it did to the waves when Jesus said, "Peace, be still!" We grow calm when we are around Jesus' peace. Psalm 119 explains that we have Great Peace when we love God's law. Jesus kept telling people to "go in peace" if they wanted healing and happiness.

God makes His children into one big family. He knows that we must all have peace with one another or our family get-togethers would be noisy bedlam. He wants us to be at peace so He can be heard.

Peace for God's children is mentioned in every Letter (called Epistle) in the Bible. Did you know that those Letters were written to you and for you to study? Paul and Peter and John and James and Jude all sent you their "best wishes" for you to receive and enjoy God's *peace*! They did not know that *you* would be born someday, but God did; so He told the apostles in His family to include you in their greetings. Someday soon you can thank them when we all meet around the banquet table for Jesus' wedding feast!

In the meantime we children can use this peace to wipe away all our problems, our worries, our fears, our anxieties, and even our tantrums! That is what it is for—to make rough places smo-o-o-o-o-oth.

I have talked to many Christian youngsters whose lives could have been ruined by sudden accidents or tragedies in their homes if they had not known Jesus as their Helper. They told me that they could do nothing but pray; *so they did*! And God gave them so much peace that they were able to help even grown-ups overcome their grief. The Bible prophesies that Jesus would come to "guide our feet into the path of peace" (Lk. 1:79). And He does.

*How beautiful are the feet of them that preach the gospel of peace...*                                    Romans 10:15b KJV

### Fruit Flavor #4: LONGSUFFERING

This flavor is tart! It stings for a while. It smarts much more than we wish. Out west we might say that this fruit of the Spirit is a hot chili!

Jesus understands us so well that He wants us to learn the joy of being *patient*. He knows that the best things for us are worth *waiting for*. He also knows that He must test our faith in Him in order for it to grow.

And above all, He knows that we cannot help other people out of their troubles until we have had some ourselves.

That is why His Spirit allows us to learn how to be patient the hard way (called the Fruit of Longsuffering). It makes us grow up every time we are given a new problem to solve. Jesus is the Great Teacher, and He knows what will help each child of His to become a better lamb. Once we have learned His perfect answer, we can tell everybody what King David discovered: "Surely goodness and mercy shall follow me all the days of my life... ."

Longsuffering is really a very special fruit. It makes us *grow* stronger so we can help ourselves and our neighbors to follow God's will. St. Paul knew all about longsuffering: he discovered that his Heavenly Father was really:

> *...the Father of compassion and the God of all comfort, who comforts us in all our troubles, so that we can comfort those in any trouble with the comfort we ourselves have received from God. For just as the sufferings of Christ flow over into our lives, so also through Christ our comfort overflows.*
>
> 2 Corinthians 1:3-5

God has other ways, too, of teaching His lambs patience. If they are stubborn, He lets them wait a while before He feeds them. If they are greedy, He makes them wait at the end of the line. If they are angry at each other, He places them in a quiet corner till they calm down. If they try to jump too far and break a leg, He makes them sit around the sheepfold until the break is healed. Lambs are famous for being rather dumb, so the Shepherd uses many ways to teach them the *patience* to *follow* Him instead of running off in all directions. He says that when His sheep "know His voice" their lessons are about over, because His lambs will then follow where He leads them, once they learn to listen.

Isn't it comforting that even Jesus learned patience in order to save us?

> *The Lord is...patient with you, not wanting anyone to perish, but everyone to come to repentance.*                    2 Peter 3:9

The fruit of longsuffering turns out to be the *spice of life*, doesn't it? It adds flavor to each day once we learn how to be patient.

### Fruit Flavor #5: GENTLENESS

When the Spirit chose this fruit for us, He probably selected the most *delicate* flavor He could find. It "butters" our behavior. Gentleness flavors our whole personality and molds our attitude into that of children whom God is proud to call His own.

One of the first traits we notice about Jesus is His gentleness. He ordered His disciples to allow "the little children to come to Me...for the kingdom of God belongs to such as these." He laid His powerful hands upon their heads and gently blessed them. He spoke gentle words of love and hope and mercy and tenderness to the milling crowds on the hillsides.

King David praised the Lord for being "my strength and power...and Thy *gentleness hath made me great*" (2 Sam. 22:33,36 KJV).

As God's children we must use our strength that God gives us (both our muscles and our minds) with great gentleness lest we hurt someone. It is a sign of power when a strong person is gentle. People respect that kind of self-control that comes from using Jesus as our example. Gentleness is a wonderful fruit.

### Fruit Flavor #6: GOODNESS

Children instantly like a good flavor. In fact, the first question that youngsters ask about any fruit is this: "Mommy, does it taste good?" I notice that most kids want someone else to make that decision for them! I often wondered in the newborn nursery what would happen if these little infants heard someone say that milk was bad; would they stay hungry rather than try out their own little tasters?

Perhaps that is what happens so often about goodness. Kids don't want to try being good until they have tried being naughty. Goodness is one fruit that lies around unnoticed; yet, it is the *pick of the crop*! Our old natures tell us to "raise Cain" first so we won't "miss any fun." Then when we can't get away with "it" any longer, we'll start being good. Right, kids?

Wrong! God is looking into our hearts all the time in hope of seeing His fruit growing there. If His goodness is not present, then the other fruits are missing too. The Bible says that only bitter fruit can grow in a bad heart; it is called "sour grapes" or "wild grapes" that put the teeth "on edge." God says that these vines (bitter people) will be pulled and burned up.

God has a great deal to say about goodness because He is the one *good* God. The Bible says, "Taste and see that the Lord is good...for thou, Lord, art good, and ready to forgive...for the Lord is good; His mercy is everlasting...Oh, that men would praise the Lord for His goodness...[for He] filleth the hungry soul with goodness." We are told that "the fruit of the Spirit is in all [respects] *goodness*..." (Eph. 5:9 KJV).

When God's children discover that happiness is the result of goodness at work *inside* them, they experience the *newness* of life that makes living worthwhile. Unhealthy habits are discarded. Drugs and alcohol and nicotine become unnecessary chemicals to produce highs or lows. Instead, they get their *highs* from the *joy* of the Lord which comes from being in love with the only *good* God, the King of Kings.

God's goodness is "fulfilling," "rich," "enduring," "great," "satisfying," "blessing"; it makes folks "rejoice," "glad in heart," "merry," "praising," and even "fear and tremble" at its greatness! God's Word says so. It is a fruit worth tasting—*over and over*.

### Fruit Flavor #7: FAITH

This is the *exciting* flavor. Perhaps an apple best describes it. Each is full of seeds, just waiting to be sown. Each brings forth fruit in its season. Even at other times we find that both *faith* and apple trees serve as shade and shelter and dwellings for God's creatures. When *faith* and apple trees are in bloom, they bring joy to all who see them!

That must be why God's Word says so very much about *faith*:

> ...*think soberly, according as God has dealt* [handed] *to every man the measure of faith.*          Romans 12:3 KJV

> *And without faith it is impossible to please God, because anyone who comes to Him must believe that He exists and that He rewards those who earnestly seek Him.*          Hebrews 11:6

*Now faith is being sure of what we hope for and certain of what we do not see.* Hebrews 11:1

The story of a Yankee youngster named Johnny Appleseed was told to me as a little boy. Johnny decided to walk westward because he loved the fields and trees and blue skies. He had collected a bagful of apple seeds which he scattered along the way, leaving a trail of future apple trees behind him wherever he went. They were his seeds of faith that could help feed others years after Johnny had passed by.

## With Faith Comes Power

Jesus told His disciples that *faith* is so powerful that even a little "pinch" of it could *move a mountain*! He held a tiny seed of mustard in His hand to show them what He meant. He told a sick woman one day, when she reached out and touched His gown, "your faith has healed you"—and the bleeding stopped. He told another lady whose daughter had a devil in her that her faith (in asking Him for help) had already cast out the devil; she went home and found the girl well already! The Lord told Peter who was amazed to see an unfruitful tree wither when Jesus rebuked it one day. "Have faith in God...whatever you ask...believe that you have received it, and it will be yours."

The Bible tells us that *faith* in God—

purifies us—Acts 15:9
saves us—Luke 18:42
makes you well—Luke 17:19
sanctifies—Acts 26:18
justifies—Romans 3:28
unites us—Ephesians 4:13

establishes us—Colossians 2:7
edifies us—1 Timothy 1:4
pleases God—Hebrews 11:6
develops patience—James 1:3
saves the sick—James 5:15
overcomes the world—1 John 5:4

### Faith Is A Tender Plant

When children ask God the Father for the gift of His faith, He gives them one of His seeds of faith to be planted in their hearts. From then on they must take good care of it, like a tender plant! God's *plant food* is His gospel; children who feed their seed of faith with God's Word every day discover that their little kernel of faith grows new leaves and roots, "from faith to faith" (Rom. 1:17 KJV). Very soon they can "live by faith" because Jesus promises: "If you believe, you will receive whatever you ask for in prayer" (Mt. 21:22).

The Bible warns us that "little faith" and "weak faith" won't work well; it acts like wet spaghetti—no strength, no power. Again, the Bible warns that faith without love is "nothing" and faith without works is "dead." We are told that our faith in God does nobody any good if we fail to love and help others. That is something important to remember! We must practice sharing and showing our faith if we are to find the joy and excitement of knowing Jesus as our Lord.

### Fruit Flavor #8: MEEKNESS

Meekness is not weakness! The Spirit would not give us "weak fruit," would He? When the Bible refers to *meekness*, God uses the Greek word meaning *mildness, humility, gentleness*. That describes Jesus' nature.

He was mild-mannered even when standing before Pilate and the howling mob. His answers were gentle. He remained humble all His life because He was already a King and did not have to prove it. "For I *am meek...*" (Mt. 11:29b KJV).

And now we are learning that the Spirit of God gives us the same fruit of *meekness* that Jesus had. What a lovely gift to share with those around us.

When St. Paul had to write a stern letter to young Christians (who were being poor witnesses for God), he said:

*By the meekness and gentleness of Christ, I appeal to you...*
                                        2 Corinthians 10:1

The prophet Zephaniah urged his people to—

*Seek ye the Lord, all ye meek of the earth...seek righteousness, seek meekness: it may be ye shall be hid in the day of the Lord's anger.*          Zephaniah 2:3 KJV

God's children, even the grown-ups, do not always act as honestly and kindly as they should to one another. When this happens, the Bible tells us what to do and how to do it if we are "spiritual persons":

*Brethren, if a man be overtaken in a fault, ye who are spiritual, restore such an one in the spirit of meekness; considering thyself, lest thou also be tempted. Bear ye one another's burdens, and so fulfil the law of Christ.*
                                        Galatians 6:1-2 KJV

God's purpose in giving us the fruit of meekness is obvious: We are to use it to restore friendships. St. Paul says to "...live a life worthy of the calling you have received. Be completely humble and gentle; be patient, bearing with one another in love" (Eph. 4:1-2). When we wish to teach someone, we are told to do it with meekness and patience (2 Tim. 2:25). St. Peter tells young Christians to be ready at all times to give an answer to everyone who asks why they have hope, but to do it "with meekness and fear (respect)."

Now we can understand why the Spirit gives us meekness; it gets results without a fight.

### The Last Flavor #9: TEMPERANCE

As a little boy I never heard the word *temperance* used except when someone was talking about Carrie Nation and her barrel-breaking efforts to stop alcoholism.

I suppose that no child today has heard of her or the Temperance Movement. As for alcohol, kids now ask, "So what, we sneak it into school, for kicks!" After all, if people do not have any fruit of the Spirit, they will be ignorant about temperance.

In God's Word, temperance means self-control; that means "not getting out of control." Strong people like to control themselves. They want to control situations too. That is what God wants us to do. When we have Jesus' joy we have His strength, for "the joy of the Lord is your strength." He gives us victory, and victory tastes *sweet*.

Now we know why temperance was left till last in the list of fruits. It would be the *dessert*. It is the ice cream on God's menu for His children. He is showing us how highly He regards self-control. Without it, nothing else works right.

### Temperance Takes Will Power

Of course, temperance or self-control does not refer only to whiskey. *It includes all our desires and activities* which could get out of hand if we let them. God would have us be moderate in all things. That means, don't go overboard, whether it is eating candy, swallowing Cokes and fries, watching TV, staying out late, playing Pacman or pinball; or whether it is sitting in a corner, moping around, day-dreaming, or plotting meanness. All these things lead to excesses, sorrow, and diseases.

God's Word tells us that our Creator has given us a power; it's called *will power*. We are not to act like jellyfish that are washed along with the tide; nor are we to be like fossils whose minds and bodies have died. He has given this *will* to us for making everyday decisions, yes or no. Then we are given God's best Gift, His Holy Spirit, to guide us in what we should do. When we follow God's leading, we start to bear this much-needed fruit in our lives. Isn't it exciting how He has it all worked out so it is possible for a child of His to bear good fruit?

### God's Great Fruit Bowl

Now we know about these wonderful fruits of the Spirit of God, just as St. Peter did so long ago. He was one of the first men on earth to receive them from God (at Pentecost). He is an authority on how they work together for our good.

Let's read from the Good News Bible what this fisherman named Peter had to say about these precious gifts which bring forth fruit:

**God's call to share:** *God's divine power has given us everything we need to live a truly religious life through our knowledge of the one who called us to share in His own glory and goodness. In this way He has given us the very great and precious gifts He promised, so that by means of these gifts* *you may escape from the destructive lust that is in the world, and may come to share the divine nature.*

**Adding fruit to fruit:** *For this very reason do your best to add goodness to your faith; to your goodness add knowledge; to your knowledge add self-control; to your self-control add endurance; to your endurance add godliness; to your godliness add brotherly affection; and to your brotherly affection add love.*

**Living abundantly:** *These are the qualities you need, and if you have them in abundance, they will make you active and effective in your knowledge of our Lord Jesus Christ.*

2 Peter 1:3-8 TEV

## How To Share Fruit

Some of the happiest children I have ever met came walking and jumping up the street toward my wife and me one day in a tiny sagebrush village in Arizona. We recognized them as the thirty-six pupils from the new one-room school on the hill. This was their first time to try "witnessing" on the streets as we had recommended to them the day before. In their hands were dozens of tracts telling about the love of Jesus. We watched the group split apart as the youngsters (five to fifteen years old) went in and out of the little stores and offices along the street. They were so eager to be able to share the Good News that Christ Jesus came to save lost sheep.

Just as a little five-year-old curlyhead ran toward me for a hug, she spotted a drunk Indian stumbling out of the bar close by. With glee she held up her chubby hand with a tract in it: "Hey, Mister, this will help you lots," she said, pulling on his dirty pantleg. "Get away, you kid!" he growled. "But really, Mister, Jesus will do you more good than whiskey," she promised him. "Take it, it's free, from me!" We watched him trying to focus on the picture of Jesus and lambs as he staggered off toward his hut under a cottonwood. Who will ever know whether good fruits started to grow in an old unhappy man's heart that day? God knows: His little girl had planted a seed of love and hope. When the old Indian decided to ask Jesus to lead him beside still waters, Jesus was ready. In the meantime the children from the new school were wearing happy faces of joy and peace.

"By their fruit you will recognize them."

# Chapter 11

# The New Gifts

*Jesus answered her* [the Samaritan woman at the well], *"If you knew the gift of God and who it is that asks you for a drink, you would have asked Him and He would have given you living water."*

John 4:10

*...the gift of the Holy Spirit had been poured out even on the Gentiles.*

Acts 10:45

*...But each man has his own gift from God; one has this gift, another has that.*

1 Corinthians 7:7

*...but the gift of God is eternal life in Christ Jesus our Lord.*

Romans 6:23

*Now about spiritual gifts, brothers, I do not want you to be ignorant...To one there is given through the Spirit the message of wisdom, to another the message of knowledge by means of the same Spirit, to another faith by the same Spirit, to another gifts of healing by that one Spirit, to another miraculous powers, to another prophecy, to another distinguishing between spirits, to another speaking in different kinds of tongues, and to still another the interpretation of tongues...but eagerly desire the greater gifts...especially the gift of prophecy.*

1 Corinthians 12:1,8-10,31; 14:1

*Every good and perfect gift is from above, coming down from the Father...*

James 1:17

*...those who receive God's abundant provision of grace and of the gift of righteousness reign in life through the one man, Jesus Christ.*

Romans 5:17

# Excitement
# in Heaven

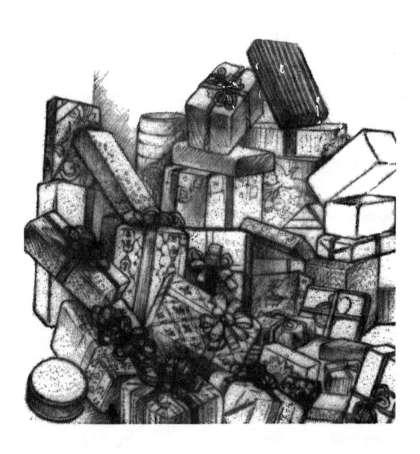

**G**od is always so busy with His Give-Away Plan that His angels must wonder if He is still paying attention to heavenly affairs! They look at the stacks of "Birthday Gifts for Born Again Babies," shake their heads in amazement and adoration, and rush back to their next job of setting the Marriage Table for the Lamb. (Right today, Heaven is abuzz with excitement as the angels scurry back and forth with their golden place settings. Every few moments they explode with applause as another sinner is saved by the Lamb's shed blood. Then they hurry faster to get everything ready before the trumpet announces, "The Feast is ready! *Come.* Join the Bridegroom!")

The job of distributing the birthday presents to re-born lambs involves almost everybody in Heaven. God the Father is the Gift-giver; Jesus is His Father's first Gift to mankind; the Holy Spirit selects the right gift for each one in God's family, and the ministering angels assist the children of God in using them. Everyone in God's big family has his special assignment: together, they work as One Body. (If there are such persons as teenage angels looking on, they are probably saying, Hey man, yah-know, that's really *neat*!" And so it is!)

Let us *imagine* some of the things going on in Heaven. On one of the huge heavenly storehouses under the supervision of the Holy Spirit is a golden sign, visible from the Street of Gold. It reads: New Gifts. A bold sign indoors warns: "Shelf Life Brief: Must Be Used or Will Self-Destruct. Distribute Quickly to All Who Ask." Other signs glow with beautiful illuminated letters that tell what is stored behind each pearly door: Cherubim and Seraphim peer through the windows and gaze in awesome wonder at "what God has prepared for those who love Him." Never had they realized that God would give such gifts to *people*. The labels read:

WISDOM          KNOWLEDGE          PROPHECY

TONGUES     MIRACLES     HEALING     MINISTRY

TEACHING          INTERPRETATION          FAITH

SERVING                    RIGHTEOUSNESS

ETERNAL LIFE

One room is labeled: Special Gifts for Twelve Tribes of Priests and Kings and Pastors and Judges. The angels notice that some of the packages are designated for "one-time use." Others say "end-time use." There are some empty shelves, covered lightly with gold dust, where packages have been removed long ago. The angels giggle at some of the old signs that say: "Words for Balaam's Donkey"; "Axe That Floats"; "Fire for Burning Bush"; "Manna from Heaven"; "Frogs for Pharaoh's Plague"; "Leprosy Remover Kit."

### The Spirit Distributes Gifts

Some of the ministering angels fluttered constantly around the Holy Spirit who loaded their arms with gifts to be handed out at a Gospel Meeting down on Continent A. The Holy Spirit explained that a big crowd of Jesus Persons had been praying and fasting in preparation for a wonderful time of fellowship and anointing by the Holy Spirit. They were asking the Father to provide gifts of the Spirit to anyone who would use them to His glory. They said that many people needed salvation or healing or boldness to tell about the Good News. Others needed to be set free from anxieties and frustrations. Some needed to have enough groceries to feed their children.

Quick as a flash, when the people had gathered to worship that evening, the Holy Spirit and His ministering angels entered and gave gifts to everyone who desired them. The joy in that little town that night was something wonderful. They *knew* that God's gifts were *real*. They *knew* also that Jesus would be returning soon to fulfill His last promise spoken by the two angels on the mountain.

> *"Men of Galilee,"* they said, *"why do you stand here looking into the sky? This same Jesus, who has been taken from you into heaven, will come back in the same way you have seen Him go into heaven."*                          Acts 1:11

Only a living truthful Lamb of God could make that promise, children. You are *so precious* that He is coming to escort you in person to your *new home* one of these days. He has prepared it especially for you, made with *love*.

# Chapter 12

# The New Home

*Do not let your hearts be troubled. Trust in God; trust also in Me...I am going there to prepare a place for you...I will come back and take you to be with Me that you also may be where I am...I will not leave you as orphans; I will come to you.* John 14:1-3,18

*Then I saw a new heaven and a new earth, for the first heaven and the first earth had passed away, and there was no longer any sea. I saw the Holy City, the new Jerusalem, coming down out of heaven from God, prepared as a bride beautifully dressed for her husband. And I heard a loud voice from the throne saying, "Now the dwelling of God is with men, and He will live with them. They will be His people, and God Himself will be with them and be their God.*

*"He will wipe every tear from their eyes. There will be no more death or mourning or crying or pain, for the old order of things has passed away."*

*He who was seated on the throne said, "I am making everything new!" Then He said, "Write this down, for these words are trustworthy and true."* Revelation 21:1-5

*I did not see a temple in the city, because the Lord God Almighty and the Lamb are its temple. The city does not need the sun or the moon to shine on it, for the glory of God gives it light, and the Lamb is its lamp...Nothing impure will ever enter it...but only those whose names are written in the Lamb's book of life.* Revelation 21:22-23,27

# Heaven—A Home Prepared for Us

Children love to dream about beautiful places to live and play, don't they? They imagine castles in the sky, and palaces on high mountain peaks. They envision lovely gardens of flowers and juicy fruit. They can see themselves rolling in the grass with puppy dogs and playful kittens licking at their faces or tugging on their pantlegs. Children can already laugh and squeal with joy at all the fun they will have in their own heaven: no broken toys, no measles, no toothaches, no poison ivy, no "come in and do the dishes," nor "it's bedtime!"

During second childhood we grandparents dream of Heaven where there are no time clocks to punch, no smog devices, no utility bills, nor hospital stays. We can imagine getting up in the morning without aching joints, upper plates in a glass, or bifocals and cane, or an old house to clean.

Dying unbelievers wonder if all the hustle and bustle of their lives was worth it. They must leave it all behind—bank accounts, buildings, autos, Wall Street—even families whom they scarcely got to know! There is nothing ahead anymore—unless it is Jesus—and they hadn't learned to know *Him*. Maybe a heaven, and maybe a hell? They painfully realize they hadn't taken any time *to prepare themselves* for the next life.

God has told us, from childhood on, to cast all our cares upon Him...not to fear...to quit worrying...to let our joy be full.

Jesus said, "It is finished!" "I have *prepared a place* for you." "On earth you are only pilgrims; Heaven is your home, with Me." "Where I am, there you will be also. I am the Way into the real Heaven where My Father and I and you will all be ONE!"

## Heaven Is Beautiful

The *real* Heaven is made absolutely perfect. Besides, it cannot fade away like our imaginary heavens do. God tells us that our home in Heaven lasts forever. It is so big and beautiful that we can never wear it out no matter how much we play and work in it every moment. There isn't even any "time" there, so we will never grow tired and need to go to bed. God's Heaven is *better than anything we can dream up*. He made it to be lived in. He wants all lambs, small or big, young or old, black or white, to be with Him forever, right next to Him. He wants to hug them every time they come running to Him to find out what to do next for *Him*.

The Bible tells us a great deal about our new home in Heaven. God's obedient, loving children will be with Him there. They will have such wonderful *new minds* (called the mind of Christ) that *they can learn anything instantly*, and can teach others down on the new earth about God.

## A Glimpse of Our New Home

In the new home we can sing beautiful *new* songs. It will not be phony punk rock music, but the *new* kind that praises *The Rock of Ages*. In fact, *He* will be sitting on His throne directing our choirs! It will sound *angelic* because the hosts of angels standing around us know the music already, and try to drown us out! The words are lovely:

> *Blessing, and honour, and glory, and power be unto Him that sitteth upon the throne, and unto the Lamb for ever and ever.*
> Revelation 5:13b KJV

These new homes smell good because they are filled with the most delightful perfume you can imagine! His Book calls it a "sweet smelling savor." It is made from the prayers of the saints, and stored in golden bowls to be opened when we all stand around Jesus (Rev. 5:8). This kingly perfume simply spreads love everywhere. (The more we pray, the more perfume God will have waiting for us, right? When I was in Paradise, I smelled this perfume; it is simply exquisite!)

Our new home will have the most gorgeous flowers and trees that we can imagine. None is diseased or deformed. Each is nourished with the amazing living water that flows from Jesus' throne. Each is glowing with the light of Heaven (from Jesus).

In our new home we discover that God has made a new garden, like Eden once was! He has lined the streets with fabulous trees that bear fruit every month. He calls them "trees of life" because they not only give food, but their leaves "heal" the nations like holy medicine!

### We Carry His Name in Heaven

We will be able to tell that we all are members of God's Family. We will have the Lamb's Name in our foreheads (Rev. 22:4). That will remind us of why Jesus could not let people into Heaven who already had accepted the mark of the beast (satan's false god) in their foreheads. Jesus had warned people that they cannot serve two masters at the same time. Jesus told them that they cannot have their names written (as born-again men) in the Lamb's Book of Life if they are carrying satan's Number or mark in their foreheads. (We must "*choose*...this day whom [we] will serve.") In other words we cannot spend eternity in both Heaven and hell. We cannot belong to satan's family and still belong to God's family. God's plan is very clear. No one is eligible to be married to the Lamb if he is already married to satan.

## Heaven's Barnyard

*Children love animals; so does God.* He made them for our enjoyment and for His worship and praise. (If you cannot yet read Psalm 148, ask your parents to read it to you. It tells us about God's wish that everything praise Him, including His animals.) In Heaven, the Bible tells us, are multitudes of animals, even special kinds. Jesus rides a white horse, and so do His soldiers. We are told that there lions will sleep with lambs, and snakes will even love children instead of stinging them. There must be birds too. Jesus said that His Father keeps track of every sparrow! God gives us pets to love down here on earth, doesn't He? On the New Earth (part of the New Heavens) He will certainly put pets even prettier and cuddlier and softer. Isn't God good?

The story of Heaven, our new home, is told all through the Bible. It is a joyful story of the home that Jesus left in order to bear a cross to become our Savior. He wants us to come home to His Heaven. God is as lonesome for His children to come home as we are lonesome to see Him! When we all meet Jesus in Heaven He says it will be like a great wedding day. He is the Groom and we are one with His bride. We then will all shout for joy:

"AT LAST WE ARE HOME!"

# Epilogue

**T**he Lamb's tale of love started long ago. The Lamb of God has been telling us through His Bible, and through His Old and New Covenants, and through His promises, how much He loves us—more than we can understand. He has explained how God made plans for us *before* we were born, and held them for us *until* we got here. He revealed how He starts His Give-Away program as soon as we seek His help. He describes how He gave His Lamb to die for us, and how He raised that Lamb out of the tomb so He could live for us!

Then He allows us who love Him to become so fruitful doing "good works" for Him that our lives will not be wasted on earth. If we are obedient children of His, He will make every day like a *Heaven on earth*!

Above all, He lets us become His ambassadors to tell others about His invitation of salvation and eternal life in Him! He lets us become His workers, and pays us the highest wages, His "unsearchable riches."

Lately, Jesus has emphasized: "Surely, I come quickly. Amen. Even so, come Lord Jesus."

### Our Love for Jesus

This amazing love story suddenly comes alive when we move toward Jesus! When one of His lambs repents (turns around) to look and listen to Jesus' word "Come," a miracle happens. All His love is focused on that listener, and the angels applaud!

It is life's most exciting experience! Little lambs find themselves with a Big Lamb as their Shepherd. They fall in love with each other, and they fall in line with the Leader. They start a love life in the Lamb, with an intimacy which the world cannot imagine. They discover still waters and green pastures. Their hurts are anointed from a cup that keeps running over. Wherever they follow the hillside paths, mercy and goodness follow along behind them.

And, wonder of wonders, the Shepherd tells them that they need not be troubled at all because He has arranged for them to dwell in the house of the Lord forever, with all His other lambs. In fact, they hear Him say that where He is they will be also, right around His throne. Their singing will be like echoing thunder:

*Alleluia: for the Lord God omnipotent reigneth. Let us be glad and rejoice, and give honour to Him: for the marriage of the Lamb is come, and His wife hath made herself ready.*
Revelation 19:6b-7 KJV

These lambs look into the eyes of *THE* LAMB, and they know for sure that "greater love hath no man than this" Jesus. He gave His *all*; now they can give Him their all. That is what the Amazing Lamb of God has been telling us lambs. It is the amazing story of His GOOD NEWS. He says to receive it and believe it so He can write your name in His Book of Life!

Please join me in this little prayer right now:

Dear Father: Thank you for sending Jesus to save me from my sin. I invite Him into my heart and life. Because You love me so much, I will obey Jesus and make Him the Lord of my life by living for Him and telling others that they need Him too. I love You. Amen.

# The Lamb's Recipe for Raising Little Lambs (Season Well with Love)

*He that spareth his rod hateth his son; but he that loveth him chasteneth him betimes.*                    Proverbs 13:24 KJV

*And all thy children shall be taught of the Lord; and great shall be the peace of thy children.*                    Isaiah 54:13 KJV

*Children, obey your parents in the Lord: for this is right. Honour thy father and mother; which is the first commandment with promise; that it may be well with thee, and thou mayest live long on the earth. And, ye fathers, provoke not your children to wrath: but bring them up in the nurture and admonition of the Lord.*

Ephesians 6:1-4 KJV

*Lo, children are an heritage of the Lord: and the fruit of the womb is his reward. As arrows are in the hand of a mighty man; so are children of the youth.*                    Psalm 127:3-4 KJV

*Thus saith the Lord; Refrain thy voice from weeping, and thine eyes from tears: for thy work shall be rewarded, saith the Lord; and they shall come again from the land of the enemy. And there is hope in thine end, saith the Lord, that thy children shall come again to their own border.*                    Jeremiah 31:16-17 KJV

*Blessed shall be the fruit of thy body, and the fruit of thy ground, and the fruit of thy cattle, the increase of thy kine, and the flocks of thy sheep.*                    Deuteronomy 28:4 KJV

# Favorite Stories About Jesus to Read Aloud to Young Folks: His Good News and Deeds

Jesus Heals a Girl...Mark 5:21-43

Jesus Feeds 5000 People...Mark 6:30-44

Jesus Walks on Water...Mark 6:45-52

A Blind Man Sees...Mark 8:22-26

Jesus Reveals His Spirit Body...Luke 9:28-36

Jesus Calls Children "Special"...Matthew 18:1-5

How to Be a Good Samaritan...Luke 10:29-37

Mary and Martha, Jesus' Friends...Luke 10:38-42

A Runaway Boy Comes Home...Luke 15:11-32

A Thankful Leper Is Healed...Luke 17:11-19

Jesus Finds Lost Sheep...Luke 15:4-10

Jesus' Triumphal "Parade"...Matthew 21:1-16

Jesus Keeps the Last Supper...Matthew 26:26-30

Jesus' Promises to Believers...John 14

Jesus Is Crucified for Us...Matthew 27:1-66

He Is Risen!...Matthew 28:1-10

Jesus Is Coming—He Says So!...Revelation 22:7-21

Jesus' Advice to Children...John 3:16-21

*May the God of peace,*
*who through the blood of the eternal covenant*
*brought back from the dead our Lord Jesus,*
*that great Shepherd of the sheep,*
*equip you with everything good*
*for doing His will,*
*and may He work in us what is pleasing to Him,*
*through Jesus Christ,*
*to whom be glory for ever and ever.*
*Amen.*

Hebrews 13:20-21

To order additional copies of *The Amazing Lamb of God* or to order copies of *Didn't You Read My Book?* contact:

Dr. Richard E. Eby
P.O. Box SVL #8155           OR
Victorville, CA 92392

Destiny Image Publishers
Phone: 1-800-722-6774
FAX: 1-717-532-8646

To order copies of Dr. Eby's other books, *Caught Up Into Paradise* and *Tell Them I Am Coming,* contact:

Dr. Richard E. Eby
P.O. Box SVL #8155
Victorville, CA 92392